Poverty and Environmental Education

Poverty and Environmental Education

By
Dr. M. Lakshmi Narasaiah
M.A., Ph.D.
Professor of Economics,
Coordinator, Department of M.B.A.
Sri Krishnadevaraya University Post-graduate Centre,
Kurnool–518 002
Andhra Pradesh (India)

DISCOVERY PUBLISHING HOUSE
NEW DELHI

First Published–2005

ISBN: 81-7141-972-0

Published by:

DISCOVERY PUBLISHING HOUSE

4831/24, Prahlad Street, Ansari Road, Darya Ganj
New Delhi–110 002 (India)
Phone: 23279245, • Fax: 91-11-23253475
e-mail: dphtemp@indiatimes.com

Printed at:

Amit Enterprises, Delhi

Preface

Poverty can be overcome, and that the poor can increase their income and production within an appropriate framework. Part of that framework is made up of a flow of resources and local-level institutional development, and there is considerable scope for improvement in both. However, the impact of investment and organisation is strictly determined by the nature of the policy environment. While project and programmes can bring some relief to the rural poor, substantial change needs a strong policy commitment. While the poor can overcome poverty, they will not be able to until this becomes a major focus of national policy and action. In the main, this sort of commitment has not been made in the past at the expense of both the poor and overall development in many areas.

The current state of India is highly contradictory. On the one hand, there is proclamation of a new order; on the other, increasing value is given to sectional and short-term national and group interests. With an overt concern with the India's poor goes an equal weight given to concern with economic mechanisms and relations that pay little attention to poverty and foster more inequality. The dangers of this situation are real. The lack of concrete attention being given to change will mean greater economic polarisation. Greater polarisation among the better-off, and between the better-off and the poor means instability and a lack of consensus, a lack of legitimacy.

Poverty is far-reaching, and ought to be curtailed. In a period in which resources everywhere appear restricted, this seems not to be an attractive proposition at the particle level. Welfare is every where giving way to production as an imperative, just as public expenditure is giving way to private accumulation. Poverty alleviation does not appear to be an idea whose time has come. The objections are great, but they are also misplaced. Poverty alleviation is not necessarily a drain upon accumulation, and it is not primarily a public activity. Poverty alleviation is primarily the activity of the poor themselves, and their progress necessarily involves productive expansion. If this potential for private expansion has not been realized, it is not because of the nature of the poor, it is because of the way in which national economic affairs have been organized. Economic policy has been oriented towards the better off not infrequently at the expense of the poor. Given the historic association between wealth and power, the definition of development in terms of the large and the wealthy is hardly surprising.

There is the possibility of associated growth involving both large-scale and small-scale production, the better-off and the poor. The realisation of this possibility might result from a new social compact. This social compact is not a commitment to social safety nets and welfare, both of which seem to presuppose that the poor are somehow necessarily out of the growth field. It is a commitment to abolishing artificial and onerous terms of exchange that discriminate against the poor, to investing resources where there are real opportunities for gain, irrespective of whether the economic agents concerned are rich or poor, and to creating the space for the poor to organize to pursue their social and economic interests.

There is a need for a new growth model consistent with new social realities. While the 1980s was period of clearing away many of the obstacles to development, it was not a period in which there emerged a clear vision of what represented the positive basis for growth, beyond, that is, a general prescription of market-driven operations. The model must pass from admonition to positive prescription to fuel growth by integrating the poor in their rightful place in the production function. It must redefine the possition of public expenditure in the development process, and seek to establish market structures which are both equitable and open to the participation of the economically weaker elements of the population. Most of all it must revalue the position and contribution of the poor and small-scale producers in the growth process, particularly in the agricultural sector, but not exclusively agriculture.

This means that the issue is not so much one of less government, but of government, both national and local, finding a new rationale for action, including, *inter alia*, creating conditions that will effectively unleash the productive potential of the poor.

Financial flows to the poorest Indian are not likely to undergo a very major expansion, especially through private channels. Development will rely very much on the mobilisation of their own resources, and many of these resources in the hands of the poor, are, indeed, not only the human capital embodied in the poor but also their assets which, while small, individually are cumulatively important in India. The growth model for the 1990s will have to embrace that fact, and build upon it. The paradox of most development models is that they have emphasized the value of what Indians do not have, while devaluing what they have: capital intensity has been promoted in situations of scarcity of capital, at the expense of abundant labour and of low-cost methods of manifold increase of the productivity of assets of which the poor do dispose. In a not very indiret way, the creation of poverty has been subsidized. Poverty alleviation is neither a special topic nor a low-cost substitute for growth. Is is neither more nor less "social" than development in general. It is part of the formulation of any sustainable strategy of economic development. In the 1990s it may, and perhaps should, become the dominant issue, not as an alternative to the structural reorganisations of the 1980s, but as a means of filling a growth framework with substance.

Dr. M. Lakshmi Narasaiah

Contents

1

Rural Poverty in India

"It is morning in a remote farming area in India. As her husband harnesses a bullock to plough their field, a woman pounds the grain she will use for the day's main meal. Three kilometres away, their children are collecting fuel wood and water before starting their morning walk to school".

"After school, they help their mother light a fire with a few sticks, milk the cow and collect the sundired grain. That evening, as the family rests around the hearth, father worries about how to sell his onions before they spoil and the price falls. Before sleeping his wife prepares a basket of home-grown vegetables to sell next day at the villages market five kilometres away. With the takings, she hopes to buy a kerosene lamp although she might not have enough cash left to buy the kerosene immediately.."

That description of rural life is a daily reality for hundreds of millions of families throughout India. Rural poverty, 1990s means subsistence on the meagre earnings of wage labour or unreliable harvests from small plots of land. It means raising a family without safe drinking water or proper sanitation, suffering disease or injury without medical assistance. In time of unemployment or crop failure, it means living with the pangs of hunger and the risk of death by famine.

Inside the Poverty Trap

Poverty in rural India is created and perpetuated by a number of closely interlinked socio-economic processes.

1. Policies and institutional arrangements biased against the poor exclude them from the benefits of development, frustrate their productive potential and accentuate the impact of other poverty processes.

Institutional processes that perpetuate rural poverty include lack of access to land, inequitable share-cropping and tenancy arrangements, poor markets, limited access to credit, inputs and technology, and ineffective extension services. Other constraints are lack of training facilities, inadequate research related to smallholder farming systems, and last but not least a lack of grassroots institutions needed to foster people's participation.

Policy and institutional biases have short and long-term impact. In the short term, the poor are unable to earn enough to meet nutritional requirements or to take advantage of the market. "In the longer term, poor households continue to lag behind because they do not generate a surplus for investment, nor do they have access to investment opportunities. Moreover, the rural poor may be forced to overuse resource, which undermines productivity and income".

2. Even today dualistic agrarian structure originating in colonial times persist. In India, highly capitalised large and medium-sized farms have virtually monopolistic control over land and labour at the expense of the small farm sector. Large scale commercial producers control the best farm land. Resources have been funnelled into irrigated plantations producing cotton and mechanized cultivation of sorghum. In marginal area, mechanisation has led to environmental degradation and the loss of seasonal grazing and stock routes for pastoralists.

"Thus, side by side with modern agriculture, millions of marginal farmers and herdsmen far below the poverty line". This dualism severely limits their capacity to grow food and accumulate capital. They lack marketable surpluses, and incentives and opportunities to save and invest.

3. Rapid population growth can cause and perpetuate rural poverty by increasing pressure on limited productive resources, social services and employment, as well as paradoxically-creating labour shortage through outmigration.

The most obvious consequence of rapid population growth is that, even with relatively high rates of economic growth, improvements in living conditions are limited. Total saving in the economy declines, leaving fewer resources for investment in human development. Negative consequence are most acute in rural areas. Growing population often combined with traditional laws of inheritance has led to fragmentation of holdings, degradation of crop and pasture land, and falling yields. In areas with unequal distribution of land, rapid population growth has accelerated proletarisation of the rural work force and reduced incomes.

4. Rural poverty malnutrition and undernutrition are closely linked to environmental degradation. Poor people in marginal areas are destroying natural resources as they struggle to keep their production system sustainable. In acute shortage of arable land has forced farmers to reduce the length of fallow periods and plough up land previously reserved for grazing. These practices have led to declining yields, soil depletion and further impoverishment. Population pressure is pushing weaker members of the rural community into ecologically vulnerable areas.

Degradation of the environment is strongly linked to house-hold food insecurity and lack of fuel. Much of the fragile forest cover has been destroyed by poor rural people in the search for grazing land and fuel wood.

Government policies have also wrought environmental damage. A rapid expansion of areas under crops often accelerates deforestation and land degradation. Programmes to expand cereal production into marginal areas, subsidized capital to support commercial operations subsidies for inappropriate technologies and excessive transfer of income out of the agricultural sector may undermine the sustainability of smallholders and pastoralists' production systems.

Inadequate public investment in off-farm employment and infrastructure, a lack of price incentives and inadequate access to modern agricultural inputs and services discourage investment in land conservation, leading to further overuse and degradation.

5. As poverty undermines traditional social bonds, the marginalisation of women has become a fact of rural life in India. With little or no access to land, million of women depend on casual employment on meagre wages. Often, they farm fragmented plots of poor quality. Limited access to inputs, extension, training and credit limits, in turn, their ability to enter commercial agriculture.

The exodus of males in search of work in urban areas (itself an indicator of poverty) has serious consequences for the women they leave behind. Output from land often falls and less attention is paid to maintenance, setting the stage for a long-term decline in productivity. Many female headed households have abandoned the use of oxen for ploughing, some plough and plan late and other no longer weed their fields.

6. The ethnic or cultural marginalisation of tribal or minority populations also plays a role in poverty. Many of these groups are further threatened by newly marginalized groups as the expansion of cultivation reduces the grazing areas of nomadic herders.

7. Exploitative middles also perpetuate rural poverty. Landlords exploit share croppers and tenants, moneylenders exploit debtors, and traders exploit small scale producers. During seasonal food shortages, the poor may have to borrow money at interests rates exceeding 20 per cent a month. Force to devote most of their energies to debt servicing, they sink deeper into the poverty trap.

In some cases, government controlled co-operatives and government agencies whose task is to protect the poor may themselves practise forms of exploitation. Heavy levies imposed by government agencies have damaged small farmers. Large, inefficient bureaucracies are paid for by the productive sectors of the community and frequently contribute to accumulation of large budget deficits.

8. Political troubles and civil strife have had a disastrous impact on the rural poor one effect is the disruption of development assistance to the rural poor, both from national and international agencies. Another is the transformation of many producers into consumers of social services with serious consequences for production, savings, capital accumulation and investment.

9. The international economic environment directly influences the well-being of the Indian poor. Falling commodity prices and projectionist policies in India affect the employment and incomes of plantation workers and smallholders producing for export, particularly those relying heavily on a few agricultural commodities. Change in international interest rates have repeatedly hurt smallscale producers in debt-burdened India, while world grain price increases has triggered rural famines.

The net flow of development resources to agriculture also affects rural poverty. Official development funding for food and agriculture increased between 1975 and 1982, but has fluctuated irregularly since. Moreover, concern with trade balances is diverting resources to export crops, sometimes at the expense of traditional crops grown by poor farmers.

2

Overcoming the Poverty in India and the Lessons Learned

Basic elements in the struggle against poverty in India are the provision of the economic services and assets, which the poor have tended not to receive in the past as a result of oversight or design. The emphasis on economic services and assets is just because the mass of the rural poor are self-employed, and it is upon the improvement in the means of production directly accessible to them that their prosperity depends. Health and education are very important, but offer more if combined with the material means of making a living-of putting body and mind to work. These assets and services include land, water, technology, commercial services, handling output and inputs, and credit provided within an economic policy framework conductive to their optimal exploitation.

This list is hardly new. It corresponds to the requirements of any producer. The basic points to be made in this regard are: firstly, that the general requirements of poor producers are precisely the same as those of other producer and that measures to alleviate poverty that fall short of recognizing the full range of such requirements are doomed to failure; and, secondly, that these assets and services are not typically provided in a form accessible to the poor. India has made important progress in providing a more effective framework for agricultural production "in general", this framework has not properly embraced small and poor producers. They are as follows:

Access to Land and Water

In the case of access to land, for example, land reform efforts in India has frequently involved major loop-holes, allowing the socially powerful to minimize de facto improvements in the condition of the poor. In the critical area of land rights, registration processes have been so complex and costly relative to the resources of the poor that land regularisation programmes have, sometimes unintentionally, become virtual characters for legalizing the eviction of the poor and the actual loss of their traditional rights. Irrigation without specific measures to defend the interests of existing occupants of areas exposes them to expulsion and, moreover, has tended to be concentrated in large-scale schemes benefiting already high potential areas in which the better off predominate. While huge sums have been spent on large-scale irrigation schemes, little has been spent on water conservation and the sort of small-scale developments that are more likely to be of relevance to marginal small-scale producers.

Technology Transfer

In the area of technology, attention has been focused on technologies (such as the Green Revolution) requiring extensive access to water and fertilizers, neither of which are generally available among the poor. In fact, research almost everywhere has concentrated on larger-scale production in areas of relatively high resource endowment. In contrast to this, research relevant to small-scale producers in marginal soil and rainfed areas in India has been shockingly deficient. As in other fields, this is partly explicable in terms of a frequently unproved belief that large-scale production is more efficient. It is also explicable in terms of the fact that it is the powerful who set the research agenda, not the poor. Taking its inspiration from highly specialized, large-scale agricultural units of production, research has tended to dwell separately on individual crops rather than on the interaction between crops, which is of much greater relevance to small-scale producers engaging in highly complex systems of production to maximize food self-suffícency and minimize risks.

Commercial Services

In the area of handling of output and inputs, organized services (not infrequently under public control in the past) have tended to concentrate in the proximity of large-scale producers and users of input in relatively well-endowed areas. In India the poor have had to incur the extraordinary costs of handling their own transport of goods to and from service points-frequently over long and deficient line of communication. The alternative has been to resort to private intermediaries offering goods, and buying products, at prices very different from those enjoyed by larger producers. In effect, the better off and the poor have confronted different sets of prices with the poor paying more for what they buy, and receiving less for what they sell.

Credit

In the area of credit, the situation has been disastrous. It is generally recognised that productive improvement needs a change in means of production new tools, improved seeds, fertilizers, etc. Such a change everywhere is typically effected on the basis of credit. Yet rural credit schemes in India have usually not extended support to small farmers and the poor. Credit has been concentrated among richer farmers with collateral and with demand for larger loans. In order to improve their productivity, the poor have been forced to seek credit from informal money lenders at virtually confiscatory rates. Again, the cost of modernisation has been much higher for the poor than for the better off. The inevitable result has been a lower rate of change and the consolidation, rather than the reduction of poverty.

The Victims Blamed

Although vast amounts of money have been invested in rural development in India, very little of it has reached the poor. The poor have been left to their own devices, while the better off have received a wide range of assistance not infrequently allowing them to encroach further upon the land of the poor. Support for agricultural expansion has not led to rural development, and it has not eliminated rural poverty.

The relatively undynamic performance of many small-scale farmers under these circumstances is frequently taken as "proof" that they are a poor investment. This is a variant of "blaming the victim". In fact, the poor have fared badly, not because they could not efficiently use support, but because they did not get it.

In other words, the failure of the poor to benefit from agricultural sector investments has not reflected an economic failure among the poor themselves. Rather, it has involved policy and institutional failures. On the policy level, it has tended to reflect an unwillingness to restrain the socially influential from seeking to monopolize scarce resources to their own benefit and, perhaps, a lack of awareness of the incompatibility between apparently "natural" criteria for support (e.g., the demand for land title as collateral for credit) and the particular circumstance of poor and small farmer (e.g., involvement in traditional forms of land tenure). On the institutional level, it has involved both unwillingness to give weight to the requirements of the poor, and a lack of initiative in solving real problems in providing services to the poor such as the high cost of providing services on an individual basis to a large number of small and often dispersed "clients". While there has been a great deal of lamentation about poverty in India, remarkably little has been done to change it at the level of economic systems perhaps because social welfare activities are much easier to implement than real policy and institutional changes. It is possible to do very much better not by simply pouring in more resources (in channels which at times do not even ultimately reach the poor), but by changing the framework of investment, i.e., the instruments of development.

LESSONS LEARNED

Targeting of Resources

The fundamental lessons learned are that investment resources must be targeted at the poor. In a world of competition for scarce resources, investments in rural development tend to be captured by those with national and local power—a group, which rarely encompasses the rural poor. The first step in delivering resources to the poor is establishing strict criteria for eligibility for assistance. Indicators of wealth in India vary according to the nature of the local economy—in some cases it is extent of land ownership, in others size of cattle herds, in yet others ownership of draught animals but the principle remains the same: investment in those with the least assets. In some cases, for example, where women represent a significant proportion of actual producers, this may give rise to entirely new patterns of investment.

Reorienting Institutions

The intention to distribute resources to the poorest is not always accompanied by actual performance. Among the reasons for this is the inappropriateness of delivery mechanisms. Put simply, institutions long oriented to the non-poor have tended to develop operating procedures and structures which reflect the nature of their de facto clientele and which hinder them from serving a new target group. In the area of credit, for example, insistence upon collateral in land may be an absolute obstacle to participation by the poor—just as a limited banking network may represent an obstacle to delivery to the poor, for whom the costs of communicating with a bank at considerable distance might well add significantly to the real cost of credit. Effectively channeling resources to the poor, therefore, means the elaboration of institutional means of delivery consistent with their circumstances.

However, it must be recognized that there are exceptional institutional costs associated with providing services to (and among) the poor-costs arising from the fact that there are many individuals involved, and that their individual requirements tend to be quite small. The costs of government services in, for example, agricultural credit, are necessarily higher if this involves a very large number of small producers than if it involves a small number of large producers. Administration costs in banking tend to be much higher relative to loan volume if it involves a myriad of individual small loans. These factors have often been adduced as reasons for the "impossibility" of serving the poor. Effective Service appears financially impossible, especially the context of widespread retrenchment in public expenditure under structural adjustment programmes. The poor are often willing to pay the actual costs of services especially if the alternative is no service at all, or supply by local informal monopolists. On the other hand, there are proven ways of reducing costs of service supply to the poor by involving the poor themselves. Everywhere in India poor people overcome some of the obstacles involved in their individual poverty through cooperation and joint action. While such organisation typically develops in the absence of formal service organisations and markets, it can also develop in association with formal organisations. In effect, the organised small farmer can help shoulder the cost of services through organising local level distribution and administration themselves.

People's Participation

People's participation is, therefore, not only a "social" concept. It is an eminently economic concept, involving cost sharing. It is fundamental to the sustainability of improvements. The long-term solution is not to throw money at the problems of the poor, but to help them to organise to overcome them themselves. One of the happy externalities of this approach is not only lower cost services, but services more likely to be in harmony with what small farmers perceive themselves as needing.

Balanced Development

Development means change, not only in the volume of production, but in the composition of output and the conditions under which it is produced. What is argued is that the pursuit of development without the inclusion of the mass of small-scale producers and the poor has important structural drawbacks, and that their inclusion offers the basis for more sustainable long-term development. Some smallholder groups have a vast unutilized potential for expansion. Others have much more modest prospects.

Even those with the poorest assets and possibilities however, can be helped to improve their condition. While the direct economic benefits of this maybe relatively slender, the side-effects may be great. An eventual shift of these groups to other areas and systems of production might be inevitable if aspiration for a better life are to be satisfied, but it is essential that this shift be orderly necessitating that support be given in the transitional period. This support can be either a direct welfare transfer or an investment in productive capacity. In many cases the latter may be the least-coast alternative.

The issue, then, is neither the "rich way" nor the "poor way". What is required is: an unprejudiced evaluation of the capacities and possibilities of poor and small-scale producers, and their potential role in the overall scheme of national development; allocation of investment resources according to potential and within an institutional framework ensuring delivery and profitable use; and a more balanced view of the overall social costs and benefits of alternative means of addressing transitional states. The belief is that the outcome of this will involve a reappraisal of the role of the poor in economic development, and a major improvement in the state of the rural poor throughout India.

The poor are many, their productive potential is great, but in few places is the exploitation of this potential an explicit focus of policy concern and action-although everywhere it is the concern of the poor themselves. While concrete evidence of the efficacy of systematic policy of support to the poor is sparse (simply because it has so rarely been tried), the evidence of its effectiveness on the local level is abundant.

3

The Persistence of Indian Poverty and its Alleviation

Poverty has always been with us and for alleast forty year its alleviation has been the professed objective of many strategies to improve the lot of the Indians. But the way in which it has been conceived, however, has been subject to considerable change. Relatively little attention was paid to the development of the poor themselves. Rather, they were portrayed as among the beneficiaries of development in larger systems which were to provide the dynamic force for he elimination of poverty (from the "outside" as it were). Development was principally something that happened to the poor on a "trickle-down" basis.

The simple assumption that the poor would benefit from general economic growth, without paying any special attention to them, changed somewhat in the late 1950s, when it was perceived that the poor might not automatically benefit from macro-economic development, but that they must benefit if the social stability needed for overall economic growth was to be assured. From this point there emerged a specific line of antipoverty thinking to improve the income of poor people.

The manner in which the poor were to be integrated into the overall growth process, however, was very specific. It was concerned not so much with what the poor could offer to the growth process as with what they should receive from that process. For all its merits the basic needs strategy, and the social "safety net" approach which followed it, basically emphasized the consumption needs of the poor-and not their surplus producing possibilities. On the contrary, a persistent theme in the discourse about the economics of the poor has been the need for some sort of transfer of resources to them from more productive and dynamic sectors of accumulation. In short, the poor have been portrayed as a net burden on the growth process.

It is possible to introduce an element of differentiation into this picture: given that it is rarely alleged that low wages are an obstacle to accumulation and growth, the poor who have been characterised as a burden have tended to be those not directly integrated into nascent large-scale systems of production: these are the poor "peripheral" to modern economic process - a group which encompasses a large proportion of the urban population in India (principally employed in the "informal" sector), as well as a vast mass of small, but relatively independent agricultural producers.

Implicitly, then, the concepts of "peripheral", small-scale and poor have been run together to form, in the realm of ideas, a more or less dependent mass. The number of people ostensibly in these categories is huge, and they seem to represent an enormous burden on development. They represent a development "problem", and an awesome one at that.

While substantial progress has been made in India in reducing the percentage of the rural population below nationally defined poverty line, the absolute number of the rural poor has increased. The growth of output did not bring about a significant improvement in the income share of the lowest nor an uniform reduction in the percentage of the rural population below the poverty line. The situation actually worsened less than half of the rural population in India has access to safe water or sanitation, and only 60 per cent had any access to health services. National data on life expectancy, infant mortality and literacy show improvement, but also the persistence of completely unacceptable conditions.

The pursuit of growth has not solved the development problem. Trickle-down has not worked or it has not worked enough. The massive persistence of poverty, particularly in rural areas represents a problem for the popular acceptance of continued economic adjustment; and it represents a problem for growth itself. The problem lies not only in the unintended consequence of the prevailing development paradigm, but in the viability of the paradigm itself. Part of the debt crisis arose from an inability to mobilise fully domestic assets, and from systematic resort to external resources. The unsustainability of this form of development has been amply demonstrated. Part of the answer to the challenge of development lies in a greater and more appropriate use of the resources of developing countries themselves.

A substantial part of these assets can be created by the poor who have been so marginal to past development efforts. The poverty of a nation and the poverty of people are not as easily separable as was often thought in the past. In many cases, it is difficult to envisage national growth without strong economic development among the poor themselves not as objects, but as subjects of development. The fact that this is insufficiently perceived is as much an expression of the development of social and economic interests as it is of the development or otherwise of economic theory. Development has frequently been associated with large-scale production and large-scale inputs of capital, and these new social and economic patterns have often defined development in their own image, i.e., in terms of the centrality of large-scale production and accumulation.

Poverty Alleviation

The perspective is not that growth achieved by the better off will pull the poor out of poverty, but that the mobilisation and enhancement of the resources and activities of the poor themselves can uphold their dignity and free them from the shackles of misery, while at the same time making a vital contribution to overall sustainable growth.

Individually and collectively, the obstacles facing the poor are formidable. They are, however, not insuperable. Most of the forces creating poverty are essentially social. They reflects systems of resources allocation that are made by societies, and as such they can be reversed. Pricing policies, credit systems, and social and productive services, which neglect the poor, as well as gender discrimination, are no natural, universal and inevitable facts and neither is the poverty they give rise to. One of the major obstacles to overcome in fighting poverty is the perception of poverty itself and of the poor. In this regard, perhaps the most important point is that the poor are not idle, they work. Nobody is simply "poor". In other words, it is not just a state of being. In this regard, "poor" is more aptly used as an adjective rather than as a noun. The rural poor are poor farmers, poor herders and poor fishermen. In short, they are poor producers: their incomes are gained from their work. The answer to poverty lies in creating the conditions for them to earn more from their work. From this perspective, overcoming poverty does not mean less growth, it is a contributor to growth for it means making the poor more productive. Too often in the past poverty alleviation has been seen as a burden on the economy, as involving a transfer of something for nothing in exchange. It need not be that way: It can be an investment in production, benefiting both poor and the national economy. Poverty has been defined as a production problem, and poverty alleviation as an investment.

Nobody wishes to be poor, and few accept it passively. The poor are rarely without initiative. What they lack are the means of pursuing it. In no small measure, overcoming poverty involves building upon this initiative and will, helping organize cooperation, and providing material support. This support does not have to take the form of handouts. The problem of the poor is not that they cannot handle resources efficiently, but they do not have access to them.

The challenge of creating an institutional framework for credit for the poor is an expression of the general institutional challenge facing poverty alleviation: institutions are not oriented to the poor. Many factors enter into this, ranging from the costs of working with a large number of unorganized people, to the prevalence of myths about the improvidence of the poor, to a simple desire on the part of the better-off to monopolise scarce resources. The answer to this is to create institutional responsiveness, either through introducing demand led organisation into existing institutions concerned with the poor or through promoting institutions created by the poor themselves. In both cases, participation by the poor is critical. The objective is not only to mobilize the individual initiatives of the poor, but also to mobilize their collective strength and capabilities. As individuals, many of the poor are virtually unreachable. As members of associations and groups they create their own channels for institutional access.

The poor as producers; the poor as credit-worthy handler—of material assistance; the poor as institutional actors—these are not elements of theory, but of practice and experience. Notwithstanding the growing acceptance of the need to do something "about" the poor, not everyone shares this understanding of poverty. As long as the poor are viewed from afar, the myths of poverty and the poor persist. Even those who over reemphasize the need for social "safety nets" and handouts, while ostensibly helping the poor, maintain the image of helplessness, and of the need to do something "for" them. A closer view reveals something very different: tremendous work and initiative on the part of the poor, both based on their desire to do something for themselves. This is not a burden, it is an extraordinary social and economic asset. Again, viewed from a distance, poverty looks overwhelming. The closer view reveals very specific situations of opportunities and needs. These can be responded to, not only through soup kitchens, which should be seen as desirable in addressing emergencies only but through strengthening the individual and collective means available to the poor to carve out their own path of independence and growth. The dynamics of poverty are reversible, but only in collaboration with the poor themselves.

Precisely because of past neglect of the poor as producers, a neglect involving a failure to involve them in the process of technological development, organisation, and capitalisation, the gap between the current and potential production of the poor is enormous. Investment in the poor is not a loss-making enterprise. Poverty is less a failure of the poor, than a failure of policy-makers to grasp their potential. Far from there being a tradeoff between poverty and growth, the persistence of poverty represents a limit to growth.

Mobilizing and enhancing the ability of the rural poor to expand their own income and contribute to national growth is not simply a process of raising incomes. It involves structural change in economies and societies. It involves helping the poor to position themselves securely within main-line economic processes. This means first increasing and improving their access to land-by land reform, land-titling, better management and better conservation, supported where necessary by irrigation, new technologies and improved infrastructure. Secondly, it means increasing the productivity and use of rural labour, emphasizing labour intensive technology and better training for new skills. Thirdly, it means making more capital available to the rural poor, mobilizing savings, providing infrastructure and developing financial services tailored to their situation and needs.

Not least, it mean acknowledging the important contribution of poor women in all of these areas of activity. At present, the contribution of women to the rural economy is seriously underestimate—the "invisible women" syndrome. Official statistics rarely make any effort to measure it, even though it is more than clear that not just unpaid household work but the farm and trading activities of women make a vital and significant contribution to the well being of poor rural households. All the evidence suggests that the poorer the household the more hours women work and greater their investment in both economic production and family welfare. From a situation of multiple disadvantage as poor, as women and often as single parents, women can move to one in which they contribute and benefit three-fold-in the home, in society at large and, not least, in the development of the next generation.

Many of he measure that need to be taken to allow the poor to realize their potential do not involve more expenditures: they involve the elimination of economic distortions against the rural poor. These distortions have effectively taxed the poor, and mainly the rural poor, in favour of inappropriate and inefficient urban developments whose support has been at the root of widespread economic crises. To no small extent, helping the poor make their potential contribution to development involves no more than creating a "level playing field" and, when conceived in such a light, structural adjustment can make a vital contribution to both resumed growth and social equity. It is often felt that the poor are somehow "outside" the scope of national economic policies. This is virtually never the case. They are affected by national economic policies, but this inclusion takes a very special form: exposure to the costs, and exclusion from the benefits. In this regard, there is a certain irony in the view that small-scale producers "need" subsidies to survive. In fact it has been the development of large-scale production in agriculture (and industry) in India that has been heavily dependent upon subsidisation over the decades—benefits, which smaller-scale producers have rarely enjoyed.

This is characteristic of many forms of large-scale production in India although nominally at the cutting edge of efficiency and productivity; it is they rather than the small-scale producers who have been dependent upon transfers and protection for their reproduction.

Change in the environment of poverty necessitates greater awareness of the root causes of poverty on the part of policy-makers. However, the realisation of the social and economic potential of the rural poor is not just a question of economic policy and investment. It also involves the development of a general social framework in which the economic and social interests of the poor can be freely articulated and responded to. It means instilling democratic and participatory values at every level in society and not just at the level of nationwide institutions. The most valid spokesmen of the poor are the poor themselves.

The opening of economic and social opportunities to the poor offers the possibility of more stable and sustainable change. The alternative is for societies to polarise further, for the welfare burden to grow to greater proportions and for a widening gap to develop between the modern and traditional sectors. In the end, the continued poverty of the rural areas will be a brake on the output of the advanced sector, eroding the potential for self-sustaining growth.

4

The Dynamics of Rural Poverty in India

Poverty is homogeneous only when considered from the point of view of income or consumption: the uniformity the poor as a category exists only on the level of the fact that they have little to consume. When considered from the point of view of production, i.e., the circumstances in which the poor must operate to gain their income, the conditions of poverty are extraordinary diverse. A concrete grasp of these diverse circumstances is the first step in developing relevant instruments to address not only the problems of the poor, but also the challenge of taking advantage of the opportunities available to them.

The conventional means of measuring economic progress, such as Gross National Product per cpita, tell us little about the real nature of poverty. In recent years this sort of yardstick has been supplemented by measurements of food security, income distribution, and social development (encompassing health and education). These offer the possibility of composite indices, allowing the development of more rounded characterisations and comparison of poverty at the national level. However, these principally refer to the symptoms of poverty, not to the relational factors generating it. Poverty is not a state of being, it is the effect of dynamic processes. While it is important to know where poverty is greatest, it is critical to know why it exists. This inquiry necessarily leads away from the nature of the poor as individuals to the nature of their social and physical environment. Poverty is not only a personal phenomenon, it is a social status. As such, while its effects can be measured on the level of the individual, its causes must be sought elsewhere. From the point of view of poverty alleviation the process of becoming is just as important as the state of being.

At the heart of poverty is the inadequate access of the poor to productive resources. Low incomes tend to reflect inadequate means of production, not incompetent producers. However, poverty in India is not simply a reflection of private resources. A broad range of "external" factors impinge on incomes, among them the following:

National Policies

One of the ironies of Indian development is that while no government wants poverty, many policies contribute to it—what is given in anti-poverty programmes is drained away by other policies. The poor do not always come out ahead in the balance—they are often net "donors" to the rest of society. Frequent reference is made to unsustainable forms of development—to urban over-expansion, industrialisation based on subsidies, and to public sector engorgement. What is less frequently realised is that the bill for these phenomena is often presented to the rural poor. Taxation of exports to sustain sectors with little export potential of their own and subsidised food imports to supply the urban population are policies that are often paid for by the rural poor. In many areas of India, exports are agricultural goods produced by small farmers. Here export taxes contribute to rural poverty. The same is true of "cheap" food imports which depress the prices paid to small farmers for their food crops.

"Structural imbalance" is not only a recipe for increasing external indebtedness, it is also a recipe for increasing the poverty of the rural population. The political weakness of the poor in most areas is not only the basis for inadequate poverty alleviation programmes and policies—it is the basis for an actual transfer of their income to more socially influential groups. While it is often correctly asserted that the poor are the first to suffer from adjustments involving public social expenditure cuts it is often the case that they also have the most to gain from the elimination of policy-based economic distortions that reflect social power rather than productive efficiency and potential.

Demographic Factors

Accelerated population growth is a long-term contributor to poverty. In India the incomes of the poor have declined, mortality rates are also falling, pushing the numbers up. In the meantime, land is becoming scarcer, plots more fragmented and the soil and pasture increasingly degraded. This phenomenon is not without its policy dimensions. As long as the poor remain undercapitalised, and essential determinant of household income is the amount of labour available to it household economic strategies favour large families. While population policy has a role to play, possibly more critical is a change in the economic environment. Access to capital and more secure income changes perceptions of the need for labour. In the medium and long-term, population dynamics are driven by the underlying productive systems. As long as the production systems of the poor remain underdeveloped, population growth remains high, restricting even the future possibility of development.

Natural Resource Management and the Environment

If poverty is both cause and effect of rapid population expansion, so poverty is both cause and effect of many dimensions of degradation of the environment. Many of the rural poor, but by no means all, live in areas of extreme environmental fragility, a circumstance often prompted by high level of control by the better-off over more stable and productive resource areas. Here the poor are extraordinarily exposed to the dangers of erosion, whittling away at an already meagre productive base. The threat is not entirely due to nature. Rather, poverty accelerates erosion. Without capital, the poor are frequently unable to invest in even traditional methods of soil and water conservation. And without sufficient land they are forced to shorten fallow periods, putting further strain on the resource base. As in the case of population growth, the result is strain not only on the poor, but on the entire Indian economy. Given the extremely limited economic alternatives, the solution to this problem is not to forbid the use of environmentally fragile resources to the poor, it is to change the conditions under which their use takes place. Access to conservation technology is important; but more so are security of land tenure and resources to invest.

Combating poverty means not only increasing the production of the poor, but also preserving and enhancing the long-term value of the resource they control. What this very often means, in practice is assisting the poor in reestablishing a stable relationship with fragile resource. Prevailing processes in many areas invovle the gradual—and sometimes not so gradual—depletion of natural resources, to the detriment of all. Part of the answer to this is conservation. Part of the answer is also to provide viable economic alternatives to the poor, reducing their dependence on erosion-prone crop and livestock practices.

Exploitative Intermediates

The poor are not unaware of the pressure upon them, and also of means of overcoming them. Their ability to respond, however, is severely impaired by social powerlessness. The poor are surrounded by a dense network of public and private factors reducing their fredom of action, and actually draining what few resources they do have. Members of the network include traders and moneylenders capitalizing upon the economic weakness of the poor, and engaging them in unequal exchanges. They also include public agencies either indifferent to the requirements of the socially uninfluential, or actively engaged in extracting "surplus" for use by other groups. Not to be excluded from this are organisations which are ostensibly "for" the poor, but which, in fact, serve as systems of containment and control.

5

Women and Poverty

It is becoming more evident that the majority of the poor in developed and developing worlds are women. Poverty among rural women is growing faster than among rural men. Over the past 20 years, for example, the number of women in absolute poverty rose by 50 per cent as against some 30 per cent for rural men. The alarming evidence concerning the underlying trends for this process strongly indicates that the gender composition of the poor is veering towards a greater share of women.

Poverty manifests itself in many ways among migrant and refugee women, elderly women and children and indigenous women. Poverty is a complex, diverse and dynamic condition stemming out of depravation with respect to income, from social inferiority, isolation, physical weakness, powerlessness and humiliation.

Analysis of women's poverty suggest that its main causes stem from the perpetual disadvantage of women in terms of their position in the labour market, access to productive resources and income for the satisfaction of their basic needs. They also demonstrate that poor women possess exceptional resourcefulness, initiative and entrepreneurial spirit and that they show tenacity and self-sacrifice in trying to take a long-term view of their poor economic conditions and in safeguarding their livelihoods.

Development is the most important challenge facing the human race. The lack of progress in the last twenty years in the eradication of poverty and growing proportion of women among the poor is the single most important threat to the progress of development and its sustainability. As long as three-quarters of the world population continue to suffer from acute depravation, as long as profound imbalances in global consumption continue to persist, and, more important, as long as the spread of poverty, particularly among women, continues unchecked, there can be no development. The history of the development process show again that the economic status of women is the key variable in the solution to the poverty crisis. It is time for the full recognition of the fact that women are part of the solution to poverty and to the stagnating development, not part of the problem.

The Earth Summit in Rio, the Human Rights Conference in Vienna, the Population Conference in Cairo and the Beijing conference all were milestone events in terms of advancing our understanding of the crucial role of women in the work place and in society. All of them drew attention to women's full and effective participation in development. None. however, full articulated how to achieve this challenging task.

It is important to retain focus on the issue of economic potential when discussing poverty among women because it is clear that power is only meaning something in practical terms if it is reinforced by economic power. Women have the means to transform productive resources into such power if only enabling environment is created. It is not the lack of capabilities, but that of resources, which is clearly responsible for women's poverty.

Sometimes the so badly needed resources are not even truly scarce. Billions have been wasted on arms purchases around the globe and particularly in the countries, which can not afford such misallocation of public funds. At the same time, wome's organisations from grassroots to the international level are poorly funded. Such misallocation of resources at the time when poverty among women is increasing is immoral and unacceptable, not only on the part of the governments, which pursue such wasteful policies, but also on the part of the suppliers, who in most cases are developed economies.

Government's responsibilities do not end here. It is extremely important, and indeed it is the main duty of every government around the world, to providc a conducive environment for economic growth and stability by pursuing responsible and sound macro-economic policies, which will enable the economy to grow without marginalizing women. When inflation is rampant, when political climate is unstable leading to conflicts and civil strife, little can be done for poverty alleviation.

6

Towards a New Policy on Poverty Reduction

In recent years, the call for the policy which enables the reduction of mass poverty in India has increased not only from scientific point of view, but also from political and practical standpoint. Mass poverty is a problem crucial not only for the people concerned, but also for the future of humanity as a whole, and one that cries out for rapid solution. Indians still have not succeeded in permanently improving the living conditions of big parts of their population. Measures in terms of economic growth expected by Indians over the past fifty years, the preliminary growth-oriented development strategies pursued hitherto have not been unsuccessful. Many poor population groups continue to be excluded from the economic growth. The "Trickle-down effect" has failed still fails to reach them.

Marginalisation

As a result, the course development took in India led to the marginalisation of broad sections of the population. Marginal groups arose that were denied access to the development process. They are characterized by a lack of active participation (exclusion from decision-making processes) and passive participation (failure to receive goods, services and social services). Such groups found themselves in a vicious circle. Because of their marginality they achieved only low rates of labour productivity and remained poor. They consequently slipped further towards the fringe of development. The greater the progress attained by the other sectors of the economy, the more acute the marginalisation process became. The numerical increase in membership of these marginal groups was so great that in course of time they came to constitute a considerable proportion of the population.

This mass poverty is unacceptable not only form a humanitarian point of view. It also engenders problems of global dimensions. the increasing threat to the environment, a population growth stretching the capacity of the earth to its very limits, dramatic difficulties in India safeguarding food supplies, and the still unresolved debt crisis are only the tip of an iceberg that is to a large extent spawned and nurtured by mass poverty.

In view of this situation it seems paradoxical that the scientific literature related to the problem of mass poverty apparently finds it difficult to precisely define poverty, to ascertain its causes and to asses it in ethical, political, social and economic terms. The literature often states that there is neither a generally acceptable definition nor a more or less comprehensive and stringent theory of poverty. However, the lack of generally binding definitions of the concept is due not to the often cited difficulty of measuring the societal "quality" of poverty in quantitative terms. The reason is rather that both societies as a whole and individual social groups with differing values, religious convictions, ideologies and the resulting structures and functions, reach differing conclusions on where the line between "poor" and "not poor" is to be drawn. Views differ just as widely on the societal and individual salience of poverty. A generally valid concept of poverty applicable to every social context is accordingly not available.

Absolute and Relative Poverty

In discussing the problems of poverty, a distinction must be drawn between absolute and relative poverty. In the case of absolute poverty the insufficiency of resources available to an economic entity for the maintenance of physical subsistence is so drastic that the affected parties are no longer able to live a manner "fit for human beings." In the case of relative poverty an economic entity has insufficient resources in comparison to other economic entities. This relative poverty does not necessarily mean that those affected are unable to live a life fit for human beings. It means merely that, due to the distributional structure prevailing in an economy, individual economic entities suffer deprivation to an unacceptable degree.

Poverty can be defined in both its aspects as deprivation. The deprivation can refer to various economic, social and/or political areas of human life. Poverty then means that various economic, social, and/or political needs of certain social groups are not satisfied, or are only inadequately satisfied. How drastic deprivation must be in individual cases and in what areas it has to occur before one can speak of absolute or relative poverty depends both on the observer's concept of tolerance and standards and on the given frame of reference.

The attempt to formulate an objective and generally valid definition of poverty must be abandoned. Poverty is a complex and multifaceted problem. Since it can be caused by deprivation in different areas, there are in reality different poverty profiles. The poor are, in fact, by no means a homogenous group. There is a multitude of different poverty groups with different interest and needs, such as women and children, the rural and the urban poor, members of various ethnic group and religious communities. The can lead not only to conflict between different poverty groups but also to discord within the respective groups, hampering formulation of consistent strategies for reducing poverty.

Varieties of Poverty

If mass poverty is to be lastingly eliminated, its causes must be recognized and purposively eradicated This is the only way to go beyond cosmetic treatment of the symptoms to provide permanent solutions. Poverty cannot be attributed to a single cause. It can always be traced back to the aggregation of various factors deriving to a large extent from the social system concerned. The divers contexts in which the production factors labour, capital and natural resources, technical knowledge, and the total environment relevant to development interact give birth to different "varieties of poverty". Successful projects and programmes for reducing poverty therefore require the fullest possible analysis of all the relevant elements and relationships of the concrete social system.

Other things being equal, the lower the per capita income of the population, the greater the extend of absolute poverty. Since this average income is in turn an indicator for the level of economic development, poverty can partially be explained in terms of the factors responsible for the economic underdevelopment of India. All strategies that contribute to improving the level of economic development can accordingly also provide an at least partial solution to the problem of poverty. In other words, a well-conceived development policy can at the same time be a functioning policy for reducing mass poverty as well.

Growth with Poverty

On the other side it has to be seen that economic growth is not automatically linked with poverty reduction. Historical examples of the last three decades clearly show that economic growth can go hand in hand with poverty increase. Even in cases where the above mentioned requirements of a development-promoting policy have been fulfilled, growth was accompanied by and increase of poverty due to a missing participation of broad segments of the population in this growth process. Or to formulate it more generally: Between growth and distributional justice defined at least as reduction mass poverty can be a target conflict which has to be solved by other measures than by additional growth politics. In fact, the more unequally income is distributed, the more probable material poverty becomes. The factors determining the interpersonal distribution structure of a country thus also contribute to explaining poverty.

For the mass of the poor, ownership of productive resources is usually limited to their own (mostly unskilled) labour. To a lesser extent they may also have property rights in land (e.g., in the case of very small scale farmers), and in material assets (e.g., simple implements). The level of education and training that determines human capital is, by contrast, usually so low that no marked improvements of their position can be expected. In most cases the poor of a society are also completely inadequately trained. With the exception of their labour, they thus dispose of no or of only very few productively utilizable resources. This is true for both the rural and the urban poor.

Their situation is made even more difficult by the fact that their resources can frequently not be used for farming or certain activities to be carried on despite adequate qualification, this can contribute just as much to poverty as repressive measures taken by big land owners against small farmers, or the activities of criminal groups in poor urban areas. The utilisation of property rights can also be prevented by the complete absence of the additional resources (such as credits of job) required to carry on productive activities, or by their being available only on unacceptable conditions.

But even if the productively utilizable resources can actually be brought into use to produce goods and services, it is still not certain that an adequate level of income will be generated. At both the national and the international level, free entry to the market for the goods and services produced is not always attained. Since there are frequent legal, physical, and psychological barriers to entering the market. In some cases, certain groups are not permitted to sell in institutionally secured markets, or may do so only subject to severe restrictions in the national context, for example, ethnic minorities, adherents of certain religions, members of particular castes.

Without a doubt, the behaviour of individual groups and persons contributes to breeding or consolidating their own poverty. A decisive role is played by the relation between the culture-specific willingness to achieve, personal attitudes towards achievement and actual capacity for performance—always with reference to underlying components of poverty.

However, the social system concerned is likely to be of far greater significance in generating poverty. As a rule, the poor are a marginal group within a social system who do not participate in the political, social and economic decision-making and development processes. This marginality is not an isolated phenomenon. It is system-related and often the very rational reaction of the poor to discriminating framework conditions for their economic as well as non-economic behaviour. If the poor are not permanently to remain passive of the alms of material aid, the marginalized population groups must integrated into the system. For this purpose, considerable structural and functional changes in the systems concerned are necessary, including a certain degree of redistribution of resources, of economic opportunities, and of political power in favour of the poor. The precondition for such changes is that the ruling elites realize that in the long run mass poverty must almost inevitably lead to revolution which in most cases generates dramatic losses also for the elites themselves.

The Poor Must Act

However, in India there is no or very little ability and willingness on the part of the socially dominant groups to carry out such changes to the system. Since for the foreseeable future the poor can expect no real support form the system that discriminates against them, the initiative for such changes—if one excludes the possibility of external intervention—must come from the poor themselves. They must learn to help themselves. Self-help is consequently a constituent element in poverty-oriented development strategies. Self-help measures of this sort should aim not only to improve the situation of the poor as such. They should also contribute to overall development by personal initiative. An awareness of making a real productive contribution to a society is an important factor in 'sciopsychological" demarginalisation. Such efforts at self-help should ideally develop within the group of the poor. Under the conditions prevailing in India, self-help must always be regarded as a group phenomenon and framed accordingly. Group successes generally provide the basis on which individuals gain greater opportunities to help themselves. If, however, the poor are unable to improve their situation by their own efforts, support for these efforts must be forthcoming. Such self-help support measures can be the object of a poverty-oriented development policy. They should most usefully not intervene at the level of the target group itself but indirectly at that of self-help support institutions, so as to avoid stifling burgeoning self-initiative efforts.

Every form of community self-help requires the participation of its members. Participation is thus not only a development instrument, but also a goal in itself, since it gives people a sense of self-respect and belongings. It should thus be an essential component in any development strategy for reducing poverty. In contradiction to this demand, the poor are frequently treated more as objects than as subjects in the development process. The consequent lack of participation in the decision-making process can even be categorized as primary cause of poverty. Indeed, as long as there is no genuine delegation of initiative, decision making and implementation, democratisation will be no more than a slogan. If development is to be durable, it is essential to involve the marginalized groups in the planning and implementation of development programmes, and to give them a right of co-determination. This participation requires the poor to develop a critical awareness of their situation. They must stop accepting their poverty as more or less inevitable and adapting their behaviour to the situation. They must become conscious of their poverty and learn to regard it as deprivation. This critical awareness is the essential precondition for them being able to help themselves. Self-help and participation are thus inseparably interlinked.

Anti-poverty strategies directly addressing the target groups of the poor and which place no great value on self-help are doomed to failure in the long run. In the euphoric development policy conviction that help for self-help was the right way, it was, however, frequently overlooked that genuine self-help can only develop durably under certain minimum political, socio-cultural, institutional and economic conditions.

If such "margins for action" do not exist, the spontaneous development of self-help rapidly falls victim to the pressure of vested interests.

Gradual Approach Needed

What goals a poverty-oriented development policy would have to adopt, what strategies in reducing poverty ought to be developed, or what strategies can be successful in given contexts all depend on the concrete form taken by the circumstances as has been addressed here. At any rate, modesty is called for in this respect. However ambitious it may sound to attempt to formulate a comprehensive policy for reducing poverty, in reality a gradual approach is to be recommended. In most cases it is expedient to restrict initial efforts to reducing material poverty, especially since theoretical knowledge has made most progress in this field.

It should always be kept in mind that anti-poverty strategies have political implications, since in essence they always amount to the redistribution of resources and political power, and the reorganisation of institutions. The less evident the impression of a "zero-sum game" the greater will be the chances of prevailing an evolutionary development vis a vis the dominant society. From this point of view, poverty-oriented development policy is always a strategy of limited conflict, and is thus always caught between the desired evolution and the risk of revolution deteriorating into chaos that seldom improves the lot of the "poorest of the poor".

7

Rural Poverty in India and Development as a Policy Challenge

Poverty can be overcome, and that the poor can increase their income and production within an appropriate framework. Part of that framework is made up of a flow of resources and local-level institutional development, and there is considerable scope for improvement in both. However, the impact of investment and organisation is strictly determined by the nature of the policy environment. While project and programmes can bring some relief to the rural poor, substantial change needs a strong policy commitment. While the poor can overcome poverty, they will not be able to until this becomes a major focus of national policy and action. In the main, this sort of commitment has not been made in the past at the expense of both the poor and overall development in many areas.

The current state of India is highly contradictory. On the one hand, there is proclamation of a new order; on the other, increasing value is given to sectional and short-term national and group interests. With an overt concern with the India's poor goes an equal weight given to concern with economic mechanisms and relations that pay little attention to poverty and foster more inequality. The dangers of this situation are real. The lack of concrete attention being given to change will mean greater economic polarisation. Greater polarisation among the better-off, and between the better-off and the poor means instability and a lack of consensus, a lack of legitimacy.

Poverty is far-reaching, and ought to be curtailed. In a period in which resources everywhere appear restricted, this seems not be an attractive proposition at the particle level. Welfare is every where giving way to production as an imperative, just as public expenditure is giving way to private accumulation. Poverty alleviation does not appear to be an ideal whose time has come. The objections are great, but they are also misplaced. Poverty alleviation is not necessarily a drain upon accumulation, and it is not primarily a public activity. Poverty alleviation is primarily the activity of the poor themselves, and their progress necessarily involves productive expansion. If this potential for private expansion has not been realized, it is not because of the nature of the poor, it is because of the way in which national economic affairs have been organized. Economic policy has been oriented towards the better off not infrequently at the expese of the poor. Given the historic association between wealth and power, the definition of development in terms of the large and the wealthy is hardly surprising.

There is the possibility of associated growth involving both large-scale and small-scale production, the better of and the poor. The realisation of this possibility might result from a new social compact. This social compact is not a commitment to social safety nets and welfare, both of which seem to presuppose that the poor are somehow necessarily out of the growth field. It is a commitment to abolishing artificial and onerous terms of exchange that discriminate against the poor, to investing resources where there are real opportunities for gain, irrespective of whether the economic agents concerned are rich or poor, and to creating the space for the poor to organize to pursue their social and economic interests.

There is a need for a new growth model consistent with new social realities. While the 1980s was period of clearing away many of the obstacles to development, it was not a period in which there emerged a clear vision of what represented the positive basis for growth, beyond, that is, a general prescription of market-driven operations. The model must pass from admonition to positive prescription to fuel growths by integrating the poor in their rightful place in the production function. It must redefine the possition of public expenditure in the development process, and seek to establish market structures which are both equitable and open to the participation of the economically weaker elements of the population. Most of all it must revalue the position and contribution of the poor and small-scale producers in the growth process, particularly in the agricultural sector, but not exclusively agriculture.

This means that the issue is not much one of less government, but of government, both national and local, finding a new rationale for action, including, *inter alia*, creating conditions that will effectively unleash the productive potential of the poor.

Financial flows to the poorest Indians are not likely to undergo a very major expansion, especially through private channels. Development will rely very much on the mobilisation of their own resources, and many of these resources are in the hands of the poor, are, indeed, not only the human capital embodies in the poor but also their assets which, while small, individually are cumulatively important in India. The growth model for the 1990s will have to embrace that fact, and build upon it. The paradox of most development models is that they have emphasized the value of what Indians do not have while devaluing what they have: capital intensity has been promoted in situations of scarcity of capital, at the expense of abundant labour and of low-cost methods of manifold increase of the productivity of assets of which the poor do dispose. In a not very indiret way, the creation of poverty has been subsidized. Poverty alleviation is neither a special topic nor a low-cost substitute for growth. Is is neither more nor less "social" than development in general. It is part of the formulation of any sustainable strategy of economic development. In the 1990s it may, and perhaps should, become the dominant issue, not as an alternative to the structural reorganisations of the 1980s, but as a means of filling a growth framework with substance.

8

Employment and Poverty Alleviation

Today the key socio-economic problem is large-scale unemployment. Spreading joblessness brings many other problems in its wake. It erodes national income and living standards, aggravating the already grindingly difficult job of promoting development and alleviating poverty. Joblessness also raises government budget deficits, increasing macro-economic instability while soaking up investment for productive capital expenditure, education, training and relief aid. And joblessness ruins lives and communities by depriving people of the dignity and satisfaction that comes with earning one's keep and making a contribution to the well being of family and society.

Theories about how best to nurture development (and thus create jobs) have shifted considerably over the last decade. The state role has evolved, in the minds of many, from being a source of relief for the problems of unemployment, poverty and underdevelopment, to being a fundamental cause of these problems through the distorting impact of its intervention on the market.

However, the more market oriented philosophy that grew up during the 1990s has yet to provide convincing solutions in practice at least not on a grand scale and especially not in terms of job creation as the present jobless economic recovery demonstrates.

The weakness of the current recovery and past approaches to economic development can be traced to the failure to consider employment as the predominant means of promoting growth and alleviating poverty. In policy circles it has too long been an almost ignored priority.

Current trends thus bode poorly, particularly as unemployment rates soar. In light of the circumstances, we need to begin re-examining some of the fundamental questions if only to find out what has gone wrong with the answers.

Minimum Wage?

Let's begin with wages. With corporate restructuring in full force on a global scale, are low wage rates required to raise employment and maximize profits? A top manager of a multinational consumer electronics group certainly thinks so he liknened the perfect factory to a ship "so that we could move it around the world to where labour was cheapest". Perhaps, but this bottom-line emphasis on unit labour costs ignores at least two other factors; namely, that higher wages can act as a screen to select more productive workers and that higher wages translate into better productivity via improved worker nutrition, increased consumption and a generally healthier quality of life.

If higher wages being these benefits (and it is an open question) should government insist that there be a minimum wage rate? Neo-classical economists tend to respond "no", assuming that a higher wage rate puts money into the pockets of some low wage workers while forcing many others out of work because companies cannot afford to pay them.

Technology Transfer

The impact of technology is another area in need of study. Technological innovation is usually labour-saving and tends to originate in industrialized countries, moving toward developing countries like India, Pakistan where labour tends to be low cost and abundant. Would it therefore make sense to slow down or somehow restrict technology transfer, especially to development markets, in the interest of preserving employment?

The answer here is clearly—no. Historical evidence abundantly demonstrates that attempts to retard technological progress bring about grater poverty and lower growth. Technology, in fact, is at the heart of the new endogenous growth theory which is very much in vogue among development economists today. Slowing down or inhibiting technology transfer would certainly dash many countries' development hopes and aggravate poverty. However, the relationship between technology, development, employment and poverty alleviation is not without its complications.

In the 1980s, the buzz word among development specialists was "appropriate technology", i.e., small-scale and labour-intensive technologies that would increase productive output while allowing an equilibrium solution to be found such that the ratio of the productivity of labour to that of capital is proportional to their relative prices. The conditions for this "small is beautiful" approach to technology tended to be best met in agricultural production. However, where manufacturing industry is concerned, the small-is-beautiful approach foundered badly when the only viable technological alternatives proved to be highly capital-intensive.

Development Gap

A wide gap has emerged between developing countries with an inward focus (which tended to be projectionist and pursue policies of import substitution) and those with an outward focus and a policy of pursuing export-led growth. Competing in international markets requires technology that is as good as or better than that found in advanced, industrialized nations. Small, therefore, is not beautiful in the global manufacturing economy where product standards are high and the elasticity of substitution between labour and capital is very limited.

The drive to obtain state-of-the-art technology thus leads to a policy conundrum: it is a pre-condition for success in manufactured exports, but the impulse to compete successfully in this most lucrative sector speeds up the transfer of technology from the developed to the developing world, thus reinforcing the bias toward labour saving equipment in developing countries and accelerating a process that is seen as a source of job loss in the industrialized countries.

Technology and Jobs

Before concluding that modern technology transfer is inimical to employment in developing countries, we have to distinguish clearly between technology's static and dynamic consequences. In a static sense, it is true that highly capital-intensive export industries may not create much employment on a net basis, but the dynamic effects of technology transfer do contribute to economic growth. And growth, in turn, generates multiplier effects in the form of demand, which stimulates ancillary production activities (like food processing or consumer goods) that rely on more labour-intensive technologies.

The problem is that the diffusion and application of technology on a global scale blurs the categories of international product specialisation and creates a much more competitive and conflict-prone international environment.

For example, we have already seen the Asian Tigers move from producing goods such as textiles and processed food to producing hi-tech and value-added consumer durables. This advance is only possible due to the growth of human capital (facilitated by investment and higher incomes) and it leaves production of textiles to other industrializing countries, like Indonesia, the Philippines and now China. But the dynamic comes at the expense of jobs in industrialized regions, like the us and the EC, which lost more than a quarter of their work force in textiles during the 1980s. In spite of job losses, advanced countries continue to produce textiles, notwithstanding major differences in the hourly wage rates for spinning and weaving and the fact that essentially the same hi tech equipment is being used in most production centres.

Protectionism

What has happened in textiles is happening in other industrial sectors (automobiles, for example) as well. The intense market competition is providing to be a source of trade conflicts, and possibly protectionism, as jobs come under increasing pressure.

For many workers and managers, the benefits of foreign direct investment look increasingly like a zero-sum game for employment, and there is a real risk that the tenuous link between overall growth and employment will break down altogether. It is hardly surprising that we are already seeing negatively affected workers and local businesses clamouring for protection in advanced countries.

Governments role

The concerned governments are suppose to carry out much of this research. The three initial lines of inquiry follow from three reasonable assumptions about the future.

- First, increase in welfare and consumption subsidies are out; investments in training and human capital are in. How can investments in human capital be directed to positive employment effects? Is it perhaps not time to explore more fully benefit schemes targeting the unemployed and the unskilled poor providing them with the type of subsidies that would enhance their human capital, improve their health and productivity through better nutrition and preventive medicine, and restore the dignity of holding a job?
- Second, given the quasi-inevitability of increased automation in manufacturing, how can other sectors (particularly agriculture and services) be developed to export their long-term potential for employment creation?
- Third, given the inevitable pressures of work and productivity in the global economy, what sort of alternative institutional arrangements need to evolve with respect to industrial relations, employment and work conditions?

Finding answers to these and other questions will require no small amount of new thinking, but parochialism or a failure of imagination would be fatal flaws in this global era.

9

Link Between Disability and Poverty

Disability affects nearly every fifth household in developing countries and is a prevalent contributing factor to family poverty.

An already poor household has an added financial burden when a disabled family member is not involved in productive activities. In the context of extreme poverty, a disability may sometimes turn into an asset when the person uses begging as a way to bolster the family income. But this is a degrading path that does not lead out of poverty.

What aggravates the situation is the fact that poverty is identified as one of the main causes of disability. This is especially so for those at the lowest strata of society who live in precarious conditions without education, hygiene and health care.

An important element of measures aimed at families living in absolute poverty is that they learn how to prevent disability. They must also learn that a disabled family member can take part in economic activities.

Increasing the economic usefulness of a disabled household member can help to reduce the poverty of many families. The income earned by the disabled person not only benefits him or her but the entire household as well.

However, anti-poverty strategies which target disabled household members without attempting to alleviate general household poverty would likely be futile.

One widespread misconception is that disabled people are unable to earn a living and to be self-reliant. As a consequence, disabled people are often targeted only for passive measure of income replacement and social welfare schemes. Active measures in their favour are conceived of as social activities and not economically relevant. Such misconceptions generate and reinforce exclusion, which in turn perpetuates poverty.

This highlights a dimension of poverty often overlooked by economists. They defined poverty only in terms of household income. But poverty also means to lack social status and to lose human dignity.

Thus a basic criterion for an anti-poverty strategy at the micro-level is whether it serves to establish human dignity. An approach, which merely dishes out state subsidies or international aid to the destitute keeps the recipients in a position of dependence.

Targeting specific groups for poverty alleviation measures is always a highly sensitive issue. It can damage the fragile social fabric and may result in greater poverty for some while favouring others. Such a risk may be avoided through a participatory approach, which actively involves the poor and assists them in their efforts to gain control over their lives.

Disabled people are more likely to be poorer than their non-disabled peers because of the discrimination, which accompanies disability, not because of the impairment itself.

They suffer from social exclusion and frequently find themselves trapped in a web of neglect. The problem is even more acute for disabled women, who encounter enormous prejudices and obstacles in their quest to participate in social and economic life.

A more enlightened society will seek to integrate disabled people, to give them opportunities to learn and to work as others do. It will adjust the physical environment to accommodate their special needs.

This planet belongs to all people. If some people are trapped somewhere, we must all come forward to remove the causes of their discomfort. At the same time we must leave our shores open for anybody who decides to join us, or any body who decides to part our company.

Poverty denies a person control over his destiny. Poverty means not being able to tell what tomorrow would be like. If we examine the situation carefully we will see that the poverty is neither created by the poor, nor sustained by the poor. It is the system of policies and institutions that we have built around us that creates and sustains poverty. Poverty is the denial of human right. Over one billion people live below the absolute poverty line right now on this planet, are denied of almost all human rights. There is no way one can defend the existence poverty anywhere. Poverty is a disgrace for the entire mankind. Because we allow another human being to die of hunger, or malnutrition, we are reduced to less humanbeings. If a particular world system is responsible for creating this massive poverty we must act to replace it.

Rescurce-wise or technology-wise, there is no reason why poverty should exist and continue to deepen and widen. If we make up our minds to wipe out poverty from the surface of the earth, the worst aspect of poverty can be removed within the next couple of decades.

Each humanbeing is a wonderful creation of the creator. Each humabeing is born with great potentials. Poverty denies any opportunity for a person to achieve any of his/her potential. We have built a world system which is in the habit of pushing people down not building them up. It creates barriers around individuals, rather than remove them.

The most effective step that we must take to remove poverty is to create a system which creates enabling conditions for people and removes the existing barriers. The institutional barriers were skillfully crafted over the centuries to benefit a handful of people.

Resource-poor nations with high incidence of poverty waste away enormous human capability each day by denying poor people the use of their energy and ingenuity. If they could have been made economically active, not only they could have contributed in the national production, they would have helped expand the domestic market for the products produced. The disabled one can be transformed into the engine of grwoth if we only allow them to unleash their capacity.

We cannot be at peace with ourselves if we know there is a humanbeing, who lives a life worse than an animal. A humanbeing is supposed to live differently than an animal. He/She is supposed to live a life with human dignity. Human dignity is what distinguishes a humanbeing from an animal. When we cannot ensure this dignity for others, our own dignity becomes an empty pretense.

There must be a thousand and one ways to remove poverty from the earth. We may or may not know some of those ways already. Obviously there are many more effectively than others. When we shall find them, how many of them we shall find, how quickly we find them will depend on how eager we are to find them. But to say that poverty cannot be overcome, directly and quickly, is to underestimate the capacity of human mind.

10

Peace and Poverty

Peace should not be understood in military terms, like absence of armed conflicts. Peace should be understood in a human way in abroad social, political and economic way. Peace should mean social justice between nations and within nations. It should mean establishment of human rights for all people.

In the new context the concept of "peace" would be the existence of a political and economic environment where each individual human beings is truly free; free from the control of any powerful person or any powerful nation, free from poverty, hunger and indiginities, each individual human being free to explore the limits of one's potential.

Today peace is threatened, more than anything else, by poverty, unjust social and economic order, absence of democracy and environmental degradation.

The cold war cloud has gone. You can feel the breath of fresh air around the world. Now there is no visible competitor left for capitalism. It is quite risky to live with a philosophy, which has no challenger. To be safe, we must go to the essence of the philosophy of capitalism rather than be satisfied with the practices, which emerged over years through patchworks of expediency.

Contrary to common belief, it is not the "free enterprise" which is the essence of capitalism. It is the freedom of individual thought and freedom of individual action, which is the essence of capitalism. It is these freedoms, which support free enterprise, free trade, free circulation of capital, and free circulation of people.

We must work out a new system, appropriate for the new world, from the basics of capitalism, not from the practices of capitalism. Many of these practices take away freedom, rather than guarantee it. Traps must go. People cannot remain trapped in places where they cannot live because of ecological, political, or economic reasons. This planet belongs to all people. If some people are trapped somewhere, we must all come forward to remove the causes of their discomfort. At the same time we must leave our shores open for anybody who decides to join us, or any body who decides to part our company.

Poverty denies a person control over his destiny. Poverty means not being able to tell what tomorrow would be like. If we examine the situation carefully we'll see that the poverty is neither created by the poor, nor sustained by the poor. It is the system of policies and institutions that we have built around us that creates and sustains poverty. Poverty is the denial of human rights. Over one billion people live below the absolute poverty line right now on this planet, are denied of almost all human rights. There is no way one can defend the existence of poverty anywhere. Poverty is a disgrace for the entire mankind. Because we allow another human being to die of hunger, or malnutrition, or common curable diseases, or exposure to climate, we are reduced to less human being. If a particular world system is responsible for creating this massive poverty we must act to replace it.

Resource-wise or technology-wise, there is no reason why poverty should exist and continue to deepen and widen. If we make up our minds to wipe out poverty from the surface of the earth, the worst aspect of poverty can be removed within the next couple of decades.

We can build a poverty-free world at a fraction of the cost of what we spend on war preparations. Nations become very generous when it comes to making their war-machine heftier in the name of ensuring "peace". Can we persuade ourselves to allocate a part of our time, money and intellect to achieve peace by making the people at the bottom the winners, rather than nations winning wars? "Peace" achieved by winning wars is earned by destroying people. The real peace can be achieved by building people, by reinforcing people, by helping people to reach their potential. Removing poverty is the process of building people.

Each human being is a wonderful creation of the Creator. Each human being is born with great potentials. Poverty denies any opportunity for a person to achieve any of his/her potential. We have built a world system, which is in the habit of pushing people down not building them up. It creates barriers around individuals, rather than remove them.

The most effective step that we must take to remove poverty is to create a system, which creates enabling conditions for people and removes the existing barriers. The institutional barriers were skillfully crafted over the centuries to benefit a handful of people.

Resource-poor nations with high incidence of poverty waste away enormous human capability each day by denying poor people the use of their energy and ingenuity. If they could have been made economically active, not only they could have contributed in the national production, they would have helped expand the domestic market for the products produced. The poor can be transformed into the engine of growth if we only allow them to unleash their capacity.

We cannot be at peace with ourselves if we know there is a human being who lives a life worse than an animal. A human being is supposed to live differently than an animal. He/she is supposed to live a life with human dignity. Human dignity is what distinguishes a human being from an animal. When we cannot ensure this dignity for others, our own dignity becomes an empty pretense.

There must be a thousand and one ways to remove poverty from the earth. We may or may not know some of those ways already. Obviously there are many more ways yet to be designed, each more effectively than others. When we shall find them, how many of them we shall find, how quickly we find them; will depend on how eager we are to find them. But to say that poverty cannot be overcome, directly and quickly, is to underestimate the capacity of human mind.

Poverty is homogeneous only when considered from the point of view of income or consumption: the uniformity of the poor as a category exists only on the level of the fact that they have little to consume. When considered from the point of view of production, i.e., the circumstance in which the poor must operate to gain their income, the conditions of poverty are extraordinary diverse. A concrete grasp of these diverse circumstances is the first step in developing relevant instruments to address not only the problems of the poor, but also the challenge of taking advantage of the opportunities available to them.

The conventional means of measuring economic progress, such as Gross National Product per capita, tell us little about the real nature of poverty. In recent year the sort of yardstick has been supplemented by measurements of food security, income distribution, and social development (encompassing health and education). These offer the possibility of composite indices, allowing the development of more rounded characterisation and comparisons of poverty at the national level. However, these principally refer to the symptoms of poverty, not to the relational factors generating it. Poverty is not a state of being; it is the effect of dynamic processes. While it is important to know where poverty is greatest, it is critical to know why it exists. This inquiry necessarily leads away from the nature of the poor as individuals to the nature of their social and physical environment. Poverty is not only a personal phenomenon, it is a social status. As such, while its effects can be measured on the level of the individual, its causes must be sought elsewhere. From the point of view of poverty alleviation the process of becoming is just as important as the state of being.

At the heart of poverty is the inadequate access of the poor to productive resources. Low incomes tends to reflect inadequate means of production, not incompetent producers. However, poverty in India is not simply a reflection of private resources. A broad range of "external" factors impinge on incomes, among them the following:

National Policies

One of the ironies of Indian development is that while no government wants poverty, many policies contribute to it –what is given in anti-programmes is drained away by other policies. The poor do not always come out ahead in the balance-they are often net "donor" to the rest of society. Frequent reference is made to unsustainable forms of development, to urban over-expansion, industrialisation based on subsidies, and to public sector engorgement. What is less frequently realized is that the bill for these phenomena is often presented to the rural poor. Taxation of exports to sustain sectors with little export potential of their own and subsidized food imports to supply the urban population are policies that are often paid for by the rural poor. In many areas of India, exports are agricultural goods produced by small farmers. Here export taxes contribute to rural poverty. The same is true of "cheap" food imports, which depress the prices paid to small farmers for their food crops.

"Structural imbalance" is not only a recipe for increasing external indebtedness; it is also a recipe for increasing the poverty of the rural population. The political weakness of the poor in most areas is not only the basis for inadequate poverty alleviation programmes and policies, it is the basis for an actual transfer of their income to more socially influential groups. While it is often correctly asserted that the poor are the first to suffer from adjustments involving public social expenditure cuts, it is often the case that they also have the most to gain from the elimination of policy-based economic distortions that reflect social power rather than productive efficiency and potential.

Demographic Factors

Accelerated population growth is a long-term contributor to poverty. In India the incomes of the poor have declined, mortality rates are also falling, pushing the numbers up. In the meantime, land is becoming scarcer, plots more fragmented and the soil and pasture increasingly degraded. This phenomenon is not without its policy dimensions. As long as the poor remain undercapitalized, and essential determinant of household income is the amount of labour available to it household economic strategies favour large families. While population policy has a role to play, possibly more critical is a change in the economic environment. Access to capital and more secure income changes perceptions of the need for labour. In the medium-and long-term, population dynamics are driven by the underlying productive systems. As long as the production systems of the poor remain underdeveloped, population growth remains high, restricting even the future possibility of development.

Natural Resource Management and the Environment

If poverty is both cause and effect of rapid population expansion, so poverty is both cause and effect of many dimensions of degradation of the environment. Many of the rural poor, but by no means all, live in areas of extreme environmental fragility, a circumstance often prompted by high level of control by the better-off over more stable and productive resource areas. Here the poor are extraordinarily exposed to the dangers of erosion, whittling away at an already meager productive base. The threat is not entirely due to nature. Rather, poverty accelerates erosion. Without capital, the poor are frequently unable to invest in even traditional methods of soil and water conservation. And without sufficient land they are forced to shorten fallow periods, putting further strain on the resource base. As in the case of population growth, the result is strain not only on the poor, but on the entire Indian economy. Given the extremely limited economic alternatives, the solution to this problem is not to forbid the use of environmentally fragile resources to the poor, it is to change the conditions under which their use takes place. Access to conservation technology is important; but more so are security of land tenure and resources to invest.

Combating poverty means not only increasing the production of the poor, but also preserving and enhancing the long-term value of the resource they control. What this very often means, in practice is assisting the poor in reestablishing a stable relationship with fragile resource. Prevailing processes in many areas involve the gradual and sometimes not so gradual depletion of natural resources, to the detriment of all. Part of he answer to this is conservation. Part of the answer is also to provide viable economic alternatives to the poor, reducing their dependence on erosion-prone crop and livestock practices.

Exploitative Intermediates

The poor are not unaware of the pressure upon them, and also of mean of overcoming them. Their ability to respond, however, is severely impaired by social powerlessness. The poor are surrounded by a dense network of public and private factors reducing their freedom of action, and actually draining what few resources they do have. Members of the network include traders and moneylenders capitalizing upon the economic weakness of the poor, and engaging them in unequal exchanges. They also include public either indifferent to the requirements of the socially uninfluential, or actively engaged in extracting "surplus" for use by other groups. Not to be excluded from this are organisations which are ostensibly "for" the poor, but which, in fact, serve as systems of containment and control.

11

For Richer, For Fairer:

Poverty Reduction and Income Distribution

Will the international target of reducing poverty by half over the next 15 years be met? Not unless growth efforts are accompanied by significant improvements in income distribution. Poverty reduction is a twin function of the rate of growth and of changes in income distribution. The research shows better distribution has as much impact on reducing poverty as had increased growth. And given predicted rates of economic growth, it emerges as the factor that will make the main different between success and failure for new 'pro-poor' growth strategies.

Over the past decade, the amount of poverty reduction resulting from a given rate on economic growth has varied in close step with income distribution. On average, a growth rate of 10 per cent reduced the poverty headcount (the percentage of people living on less than $ 1 a day) by 9 per cent in countries where income was fairly equally distributed. However in countries where income was unequally distributed, a growth rate of 10 per cent reduced the poverty headcount by only 3 per cent.

The World Bank estimates that developing countries will grow at 4 per cent per capital per annum until 2015. So the good news is that the income-poverty target is attainable provided that significant improvements take place in income, distribution. These can be achieved ex-ante, by designing growth strategies that increase disproportionately the incomes of the poorest or ex-post, by redistributing income through taxation. Many questions arise. What is the recipe for income-redistributing growth? Is there a trade-off between growth and distribution? An ex-post strategies of reduction feasible? These questions are far from new. Indeed, to a large degree, they are the very questions on which the development studies profession is founded. Nevertheless, they have been neglected in recent years. Does current research offer new perspectives? Articles in this issue of insights offer six main conclusions. They are that.

- We need a way to measure 'pro-poor growth.' The concept originates from the 1990 World Development Report of the World Bank and is taken to mean a labour intensive growth path that encompasses the economic activities of the poor. However, such a growth path could be accompanied by increasing, declining or static income inequality. Mc Culloch and Baulch propose that the 'poverty bias of growth or PBG (whether pro poor or not) be defined by comparing actual change in income distribution with the change that would have resulted had all incomes grown at one rate with no change to income inequality. This difference is compared in their report (opposite) for two states in India. From this comparison it emerges that growth in Bihar State was accompanied by worsening income distribution and has been biased against the poor, whereas in Andhra Pradesh the reverese was true.
- Growth might be expected to be pro-poor if it takes place in areas and sectors where the poor live and work. For the poorest countries this means mostly in rural areas and to all large extent in agriculture. In Asia, Green Revolution technologies were adopted by poor farmers because they were scale-neutral and low-risk. Poor non-farmers also benefited from the extra employment and lower food prices that resulted in Sub-Saharan Africa, the Green Revolution has been slower in coming, but research at Reading by Mosley suggests an African Green Revolution will help. In Uganda, for example, the

spread of new technologies in maize and cassava has contributed to sharp falls in poverty, notable in the country's North where mosaic resistant cassava has made a conspicuous difference to farmer's yields and incomes in an otherwise poor and undeveloped region.

- Even so, as many will remember well from debates about the Green Revolution in Asia, not everybody benefits from growth. In Ethiopia, researchers from the Universities of Oxford and Addis Ababa found that rural poverty has fallen sharply since the change of government in 1992, driven by market liberalisation and better weather (see Dercon, backfold). Yet those who have gained have been those with assets, including land, oxen for ploughing, education and access to public goods such as roads. Those without assets are left behind. Rural inequality has actually risen, implying Ethiopia could reduce poverty faster if policies countered inequality yet maintained current growth rates.

- People without assets might be expected to compensate by migrating or moving out of agriculture. Sometimes this happens, but seeking off-farm opportunities may be easier of the haves than the have-nots. In rural Zimbabwe, for example, Piesse and Thirtle have shown that (in more remote areas at least) those with higher farm incomes are better placed to exploit off-farm opportunities, including the option of working in town.

- In any case, migration to town may not offer much to the unskilled—again, a problem facing those without assets. The evidence her comes from China, in research carried out by the institute of Economics and Statistics. Wage employment has increased in urban China, but wage inequality has increased sharply, with falling real wages for the unskilled.

- The efficiency (hence the growth) and equity trade-off is far from clear cut. Analysis by Knight of the reasons behind rising wage-income inequality in China has revealed that some of these changes reflect greater labour market efficiency. In other words, more productive, experienced and skilled worker have become better paid. Other changes hint at new inefficiencies creeping into China's labour market, such as growing labour market, such as growing discrimination: females and minority groups find they are disadvantaged in the labour market, whereas members of the Communist Party are more likely to get jobs. Other signs are sharper segmentation, with state employees paid more than private sector counterparts and growing differences in wage rates between the provinces, not offset by labour mobility.

- The cross-section of findings offered in these pages does not amount to a systematic review of the 'inequality question' in developing countries. Far from it: here is fertile ground for further research. Even so, we are confident that it is time to promote inequality to the fore of the research and policy agenda.

12

Taking a Lead in the Fight Against Poverty?

World Bank and IMF Speed Implementation of their New Strategy

A change in development policy strategy in the poorest countries is at present being prepared with incredible speed. The IMF-style structural adjustment programmers that have been criticised for many years are being scrapped. The countries are now to take their own decisions on their paths to development. Their governments will no longer formulate poverty reduction programmes top-down, but in an intensive and long-term dialogue with societal groups and organisations. Governments and institutions of the North commit themselves to supporting these process, such as by debt relief on an unprecedented scale. Dream or reality?

New Strategy Paper

Behind this euphoria lines a new abbreviation, PRSP, standing for Poverty Reduction Strategy Paper, which the IMF and World Bank invented last year. The G-7 countries in Cologne not only announced debt relief for the Heavily Indebted Poor Countries (HIPCs) but also demanded that it must serve above all for poverty reduction. The PRSP concept was then presented at the annual conference of the two Bretton Woods organisations

The most important principles of the new "super weapon" in the fight against poverty are:

- PRSPs are papers, which describe the medium-term development paths of the poorest countries of the South, particularly their strategies to combat poverty, and by this means enlist international support. A PRSP is not only the prerequisite for granting debt forgiveness in the context of the HIPC initiative. It is also necessary for all new IMF and World Bank loans to the so-called IDA countries, the some 70 poorest that receive concessional loans from the World Banks's International Development Agency (IDA). According to the World Bank, PRSPs should also be required for all future pledges of bilateral development assistance.
- Not only social sector programmes, but also the economic and financial policies of the developing countries are in future to be aimed at fighting poverty. Previously, the IMF always pronounced that a growth-oriented national economy and a far-reaching integration in the world market would have a trickle-down effect and also benefit the poor. Now the poor are to be asked what policies can help materially to improve their situation.
- PRSPs are to be developed on the basis of self-responsible country ownership. Accordingly, development and structural adjustment strategies are no longer to be developed by the Washington finance institutions, but the countries themselves.
- The heading "country ownership" is to underline that not only governments are called upon, PRSPs should come into being in a participatory process. That means involvement of trade unions, NGOs, cooperatives, associations, grass roots, groups, political parties and parliaments. A country's PRSP should be developed in a societal debate, a dialogue between governments on one side and parliamentary, private sector and civil society on the other.

Rhetoric or Reality?

Are PRSPs the expression of a change of paradigm? In brief, if all what the papers contain is implemented in a consistent and wide-ranging, way, the chances of achieving it are good but there are a number of open questions. The answers to them will have a bearing on success or failure.

- Is the IMF really changing its policy on the poorest countries or merely wrapping its old policy in new words? The growing criticism of the IMF in recent years strengthened latterly by the evaluation of the ESAF (Enhanced Structural Adjustment Facility) programmes, which once again proved their blatant weaknesses called for reaction and is now triggering changes—real or only rhetorical? There will be no more old-style ESAF loans based on macroeconomic structural adjustment programmes. But the credit line remains, and is now called the Poverty Reduction and Growth Facility (PRGF). This will be granted on the basis of the PRSPs, which in each case must also be accepted by the IMF board of directors. How much influence will the IMF have on the design of the PRSPs? What happens if a government choose macroeconomic strategies combat poverty which go against previous IMF policy? Open questions. Moreover, there is still no answer to the question of why the IMF is at all coming on with long-term and low-interest lines of credit in the poorest countries.

Mixed Feelings with Regard to World Bank Role

- Will the World Bank use the PRSP process to expand its own institutional power further? NGOs in the North and South are viewing this with mixed feelings. Many welcome the fact that for the moment the World Bank appears to be asserting itself against its twin, the IMF. On the other hand, 50 years of experience with World Bank strategies have certainly not strengthened their trust in the Bank's ability to make a convincing fight against poverty. That is why the EURODAD network also questions the role of the World Bank (and the IMF) in the PRSP process. It says the papers should not be presented to the two financial institutions, whose power over the development strategies of countries of the South thus would increase further. Rather, PRSPs should for example, be laid before a Round Table of all donors chaired by the United Nations Development Programme (UNDP).

Ownership

- The principles of developing countries being responsible for their own development strategies are as old as it is—in theory—right. There have been frequent complaints about shortcomings in ownership. But now, after decades of development strategies being set and structural adjustment programmes being dictated from outside, the governments of the poorest countries, which in many cases have only weak institutional capacities, can hardly taken on sole responsibility overnight. In addition, of course, not a few of the countries are ruled by corrupt political elites (promoted from outside over decades) that give little reason to hope they would immediately switch to poverty reduction politics. Scepticism and critical observation is justified even if there is no alternative to governments of the south taking over greater responsibility.
- Civil society actors are now asked to help out in particular in those countries whose governments appear to be less trustworthy. A nice idea that has little to do with real life. Civil society actors in developing countries in general and in the poorest countries in particular are extraordinarily weak institutions which in many cases are totally dependent on financing from the North.
- The civil society landscape in other countries is even weaker. However, social actors in many countries could make useful contributions to developing sustainable strategies. But that calls for meaningful and lasting support, including financial support,

capacity-building, and in some countries also political pressure to gain scope for societal engagement.

It is reasonable that not only the World Bank and other official donors but also, and above all, the northern NGO partners of these actors are now giving much thought to how civil societies in the south can be strengthened.

Participation?

Even assuming there were civil society actors capable of dialogue, that does not clarify what participation in the PRSP process is really supposed to mean. Is civil society only to be listened to, or can it if necessary refuse to approve a PRSP? What impact would have on acceptance of the document by the IMF and World Bank and other donor? And in view of the great time pressure, will civil society be at all able to formulate discuss and feed their positions into the process? It could be of decisive importance for the current debate on the PRSP model to delink the urgently needed debt relief from drawing up a PRSP programme, which simply needs more time. For example, it is conceivable that there would be no great problems in granting a country a moratorium on debt servicing so long as a PRSP process is continuing and then for giving debt when it is completed. That would ease the time problem for NGOs and at the same time maintain pressure on governments actually to arrive at poverty reduction strategies that were developed in a participatory process.

Other Causes of Poverty in Developing Countries

The entire current process is focused on the countries of the south, their governments and societies. That diverts attention from the responsibility of the donors and creditors. Not only that the IMF's structural adjustment programmes to date have been counterproductive for fighting poverty (why does the IMF not admit that openly just for once?) Not only that the now promised debt reliefs are coming much too late (the debt crisis of the poorest countries was deplored decades ago!). The present strategy also ignore various other exogenous causes of poverty in the South. What impacts do the finance and trade policies of northern countries have on the modest attempts to enable sustainable development in the South? What consequences will the continuing cutting of development budgets have on the South (no one anyway ventures to talk nowadays about the old 0.7 per cent ODA-GNP ratio)? Fort the donors and creditors to now pass the buck of sole responsibility to the governments of the South and present themselves in the background as noble do-gooders may be a successful strategy in terms of domestic politics, but not an acceptable one for development policy.

13

Resistance to Change:

Why Poverty Reduction Programmes Did not Work

Poverty reduction as overall objective of the global development industry is not new. The only problem is that so far it has not really worked. Despite several decades of economic growth and huge development aid disbursements, the number of countries the United Nations calls "least developed" (those with a per capital income of less than 900 USD a year) has in fact nearly doubled since 1971, from 25 to 49. In the last decade (1990-2000) and despite all development efforts—not even one country was able to graduate from this group to a higher income level, maybe with the exception of Botswana.

Meanwhile, poverty reduction has generated its own history. This programme has covered a wide range of approaches starting from the World Banks's small-farmers-strategies in the 1970's via the costly structural adjustment policies of the 1980's to the recent poverty reduction strategies of the 1990's. Once more, the next development decade (2000-2010) has written "Attacking Poverty" on its banner. It seems that something must have gone wrong along the way. What (bitter?) lessons have been learnt from previous experience? Have they been factored into the new set of policies? Were there possibly some fundamental flaws which were overlooked, and can better results be expected during the next period? Or do the many failures and disappointments demonstrate that there is some systemic "resistance to change" by those in power in the least developed countries and perhaps also by the poor themselves?

1. What Can the Rural Poor Really Expect from Poverty Reduction Programmes?

In India, of example, 70 per cent of the people still earn their livelihood in the agricultural sector; most of the poor among them live in a kind of rural subsistence economy. People who live in a subsistence economy are naturally conservative. They are busy securing their survival and are very reluctant to take risks. Their living standard is measured in amounts of rice harvested; their wealth is measured in numbers of livestock. Within this simple framework, poor peasants behave very rationally. For example, a shift from food crops to cash crops, such as from rice to coffee or tapioca, would immediately endanger their subsistence in case of failure. Furthermore, the poor do not have the knowledge and skills to change their crops quickly in response to market demands. Moving from a subsistence economy to a commodity economy is therefore a big step for small farmers.

However, poor people are always happy to receive handouts from the Government like fertilizer, seeds, medicine or blankets. Roads, bridges and schools are also very welcome. Who would refuse a gift? From their point of view it is the responsibility of the Government to distribute goods and services in form of aid programmes as a way to share some of the prosperity of the city people with them. Nevertheless, as they see no direct and immediate benefit for themselves, they tend to take a rather passive attitude to change. Development workers have often complained about this common apathy and about the lack of will among the poor themselves to improve their situation. In the final analysis, rural development is more a problem of providing the right economic incentives for change than of overcoming traditional thinking and a conservative attitude.

2. What Kind of Incentives are Necessary to Achieve Increased Production in the Countryside?

In most poor countries the key to rural development is the problem of land ownership rights and of legal security.

As long as people do not own the land that they cultivate, they are not interested in making any investments, be they in the form of labour or capital. Once a farmer has an ownership title and considers the land as his own, he will refrain from over using the soil but shift crops and plant new trees. Moreover, he can then use his land as collateral for credits or even sell it and buy land somewhere else.

In addition to clear and irrevocable ownership rights, the rule of law is another crucial factor for development. People must feel safe from abuse of power by local elites and corrupt government officials. They must be able to enforce their basic right in an impartial court of law. Furthermore, they must be safe from land expropriation without adequate compensation and from resettlement against their will. In other words, it is primarily their very stake holdership in the rural economy that will motivate them to increase their production. Of course, the other necessary incentives are access to markets, a fair price for their products and the availability of goods and services.

3. Poverty Reduction Programmes, if not Accompanied by Parallel Institutional Reforms, Run the Risk of Creating a Modern Version of the Cargo Cult

Cargo cults spread during World War II in the highlands of Papua New Guinea at a time when several US cargo planes loaded with food supplies crashed into the hills. Suddenly, the native people could enjoy an abundant amount of goods, which literally fell down on them like a "gift from heaven." In the hope of attracting some more of these "silvery birds" the local hilltribes constructed primitive models of airplanes, sat around them in a circle, and prayed that more "cargo" would drop on their territory. As this happened in some areas(albeit as a result of the air battle between Japan and the USA), it strengthened the belief in the cargo cult as some magical way to overcome poverty at least for a short time.

There is a high risk that aid programmes under the banner of poverty reduction will create new "cargo cults" in the 49 least developed countries if they continue to carry out their "business as usual" and do not put strong emphasis on the rule of law and civil rights. Unfortunately, the setting up of reliable legal and social institutions in poor countries (which often seems to be the "software" of the development industry accompanying disbursements)is, in fact, as decades of experience have shown, the hard part of the process. But it is also indispensable for achieving any tangible results.

Why have there been until now only modest results in the areas of land reform, rule of law and the guarantee of basic civil rights? Why have people's participation and people's ownership as a strategy hardly taken root at all in the least developed countries? The answer must be sought in the role of powerful local groups and their vested interests, who obviously benefit from the prevailing status quo and a loose environment. A cargo cult promises bounty for all recipients; poverty reduction, however, means changing the rural power structure, too.

Conclusion

To insist on the rule of law, on people's participation in the development process, and on transparency and accountability, is again nothing new. Good political and administrative institutions go hand in hand with economic growth. The potential of economic development is quite limited if it works in a framework of social undevelopment and official indifference. Again the question is, who has so little been achieved in this field during previous decades? Was it the wrong medicine and why were the poor results of the aid programmes so carefully ignored by the international donor community?

Looking at the political systems of the 49 least developed countries, it is obvious that most of these countries are "more democratic in principle than in practice". Many of them are ruled by military or civil authoritarian regimes which are more used to giving orders than to listening to the grievances of the poor. Other governments, such as India, are "genuinely democratic at most levels but have historically found it difficult that political accountability reaches all levels of decision making particularly for the poor".

To sum up, it seems that resistance to change is equally shared by the cumbersome and often incompetent bureaucracies of the poor countries and the equally cumbersome international donor community, which has so far conveniently kept the call for more rural democracy and people's rights on the backburner. The major reason for the reluctance of the donor community to pursue the battle for the rule of law and the fight against endemic corruption was to avoid massive political confrontation with the receiver countries.

Would it not have been better to create proper incentives for the performance of poor countries, namely by halting loans to nations that do not manage their economies and their reform commitments effectively and increasing financial and technical support to those that do? The next decade will show how determined both local governments and donors are to tackle these problems for the sake of a better future.

14

City Politics:

A Voice for the Poor

By 2020 the world's urban population will rise by almost 1.5 billion. Cities and towns house a growing proportion of poor people, partly because of the increased share of urban population of the total but also because economic recession and adjustment policies often hit poorer urban residents the hardest. Cities are associated with economic growth and wealth generation and yet inequality is high. Poor people generally live in substandard conditions, may not benefit from job creation, and suffer high levels of pollution, crime and violence.

How can city Governments cope with the challenges of population growth and increased global economic competition, and meet the needs of poor residents/is urban Governance responsive to the needs of the poor? Are the agencies responsible for city Government, especially the municipalities, addressing poor people's needs? Are NGOs and people's organisations playing a greater role in service delivery? Or is their role one of advocacy and lobbying? If so, how do they relate to the formal political system? Can Governments fulfil their responsibilities, including poverty reduction? How can the well being of poor urban Governance institutions priorities their needs? In assessing the responsiveness of city Government to poor people, three key questions are addressed:

How can the Poor Influence the Agenda of the Institutions of Urban Governance?

The influence of poor residents on decision making is controlled, in part, by the formal political system.

Democratisation gives people a voice. However, this vote means more when elected representatives depend on the political support of poor people-where they are a majority, or are well organised, or where there is a ward-based system. If poor people are organised enough, to articulate their needs and demand a fair share of urban resources. NGOs can help poor groups organise better and provide support for networking.

Where poor people are not organised it does not mean they are politically powerless. Poor people in this situation, however, are prey to the disadvantage of patronage and unlikely to be included in formal consultative processes. For an electoral system to be truly responsive, specific mechanisms and channels, such as consultative and participatory processes at city and sub-city levels, are needed to complement representative democracy. Athough these channels do not necessarily include the poorest or make a marked difference to resource allocation, pro-poor decisions are unlikely without them.

How Can Cities Finance their Activities and Reduce Poverty?

Democratisation has not, in many countries brought allocation of financial resources or the revenue-raising capacity for local governments to fulfil their responsibilities. The responsiveness of city governments to poor people's needs thus depends, on whose voices are heard in the arenas of political decision making. Responsiveness also depends on how available financial resources are allocated and how the programmes they finance are designed. There is scope, for city governments to increase property and business revenues, and to borrow for capital investment. Whether increased financial resources benefit poor people depends on how the demands of external investors and creditors are reconciled with the demands of poor residents; the willingness of politicians and officials to address the distributive implications of existing and planned spending; and efficient transparent financial management. If funds are made available to sub-city levels of government or if expenditure can be influenced by ward councilors, the funds might then be used to meet the priorities of poor residents.

What are the Necessities of Urban Living and how can Access to then be Ensured?

An adequate income: Work opportunities should be the top priority. City governments can, however, support the urban economy in general and the economic activities of the poor in particular. Firstly they can ensure that the basic services are efficiently provided. Secondly city governments can refrain from activities that destroy the assets and livelihoods of the poor, especially eviction of informal settlements and micro-enterprises. Savings and credit schemes can be more appropriately organised at a community level and supported by NGOs.

LAND OWNERSHIP is a common aspiration for poor households. A home with secure tenure (not necessarily title) provides security, an appreciating asset, access to services, and a base for economic activities. Increasing the opportunities for poor households to gain access to a well-located plot of land is an important component of any poverty reduction strategy. Many never fulfil their dream and the needs of those who cannot, or do not wish to become home owners should not be neglected, however.

Local government is potentially more responsive to poor residents than are central government agencies, although this depends on the balance of political power and bureaucratic perceptions. The limited ability of the public sector to secure benefits for the poor from public-private partnerships in land development, suggest that more informal arrangements and the involvement of CSOs may be better ways forward.

Environmental Services: Land alone will not reduce poverty but must be linked to a healthy living environment—a package of appropriate and affordable environmental services, such as public transport, water and sanitation, solid waste collection, and energy for cooking and lighting. Rather than discussing appropriate standards, detailed issues of financing and affordability or how continued provision can be assured for each of these services, the research focused on how far decision making channels mechanisms and partnership arrangements ensure that providers are responsive to the needs and priorities of poor residents.

Collaborative planning and decision making arrangements are one promising alternative, despite, the current shortcomings of participatory budgeting. For responsiveness to the poor to be built in to such processes, local bureaucrats need to change their attitudes and working practices. Is it possible and acceptable for poor people to have to rely on their own resources their households and networks—resources that are very limited? Informal networks and links can, however, provide mutual support and access to politicians and bureaucrats, community associations thought not always present, inclusive or transparent, can play an important role in articulating poor residents views and in organising self-help activities. There is scope for formal representative community organisations, for informal links between peoples' organsiations and the power structures, and for networking between people's groups. NGOs can play an important role in developing the capacity of community organisations and in facilitating networking. Where NGOs play a role in service delivery. However, there is a danger that the resulting close relationship with local government detracts from their ability to empower poor people and challenge inappropriate policies. City governments, it is clear, cannot cope with the challenges of population and economic growth and respond to the needs of poor people alone. Only in alliance with other actors is there some hope that poverty can be overcome. For CSOs, many of which were forged during struggles for democratisation, this implies moving beyond confrontation to engagement. To form alliances between CSOs and city governments that put the interests of the poor first, poor people must be able to exercise their political rights.

15

Tapping the Market:
Can Private Enterprise Supply Water to the Poor?

Over 170 million people have no access to clean water in urban areas throughout the world. Inefficient operation of state owned water companies is at the root of this injustice: gross over-staffing and political interference in tariff-setting have starved utilities of the resources needed to expand piped networks to impoverished areas.

The failure of the supply-driven approach has led to public private partnership (PPPs) designed to shift water utilities towards a demand-driven approach. Have these changes been accompanied by improved access to clean, affordable water for the urban poor? Has PPP improved equity in urban water supply? Are the new private sector operators addressing the needs of the urban poor in practice? This article examines the extent to which the urban poor have benefited or not from this newly emerging institutional arrangement.

The 'public' approach typically provides unclean water sporadically. It requires expensive, highly educated professionals, significant subsidies and tends to service clients on high and middle incomes whilst changing low tariffs. International financial institutions have failed to enable the public water suppliers to improve performance, either through massive investment in engineering, or through capacity building and institutional development.

At the other extreme is an efficient, demand driven, customer-oriented approach, the 'small scale independent providers', delivering water to cities' inhabitants, with near 100 per cent bill collection efficiency. Promoting local employment and servicing the poor, this approach has, until recently, been ignored by water sector professionals. Lacking regulatory oversight, however, their prices are typically 10 to 20 times higher than those paid by high-income consumers connected to the network. Which of these providers are most effective at serving the poor? The starting point is to recognise the evidence suggesting that the urban poor are prepared to pay to meet their survival and convenience needs for water.

Notwithstanding the rhetoric to the contrary by some trade unions and NGOs, initial results from larger cities indicate that the efficiency of 'privatised' water utilities has improved markedly: leakages are down and net revenue is up through improved billing and collection and reduction in personnel. Whether this is due to the alleged benefits of private sector investment or the freedom of foreign operators to manage without being beholden to employee and entrenched political interests is not yet clear.

Has the Extension of the Network to Poor Communities Been Speeded Up?

Concession contracts require private operators to meet coverage targets. But the decision on the direction of network expansion to meet targets are usually left to the operators as regulatory bodies are usually formed after contract signing. So are poor communities given priority? Technical criteria based on cost-effectiveness in the construction of main pipes, commercial criteria based on pressure from property developers, and political criteria based on vote-winning tactics may all conflict with social criteria based on the pressing needs of poor communities.

Is the Cost of Household Connection Affordable by the Poor?

Even where operators do give priority to extending the piped network into poor communities, difficult issues arise over the financing of secondary pipelines, household connections and meter installation. Techniques are evolving to reduce the cost of connection so as to ensure affordability for all. These may take the form of tripartite arrangements whereby the public sector provides grants for the purchase of materials, community groups provide voluntary labour, and the private operator provides technical assistance. NGOs may contribute by providing crucial skills in team management and local understanding not usually found in the bureaucratic culture of public sector institutions or the technoprofessional culture of private water companies.

Is the Water Tariff Affordable by the Poor?

Even where poor communities have been connected, there is no assurance that householders can afford the water charges. Many have no job security or regular income. Billing arrangements need to be shortened from the monthly norm to fit the short-term financial horizon imposed by household poverty.

Property-based tariff structures still discriminate against the poor by providing far cheaper water per litre for high-income households consuming large volumes for swimming pools and sprinkler systems. Reforms should positively discriminate in favour of the poor, with some cross-subsidisation from richer to poorer households. However, where the initial life-line block is greater than average monthly domestic water use by the poor (perhaps over $6m^3$ per household a month), middle income groups benefits the most. A single volumetric tariff for domestic consumers with subsidies aimed at facilitating water connections rather than consumption is now being recommended.

This article focuses on the three major challenges for the sector in the new millennium.

- First it is crucial to develop regulatory skills to oversee this affordable expansion. The key capacity constraints facing municipalities—usually the public sector partners in PPPs.
- Second is the need to incorporate the skills of small-scale independent providers.

- Thirdly it is important to move beyond the metropolitan capitals, to where cross-subsidies are more achievable, and address the water needs of the urban poor in the myriad of secondary towns in the south.

16

Unemployment in the Poor and Rich Worlds:

Different Causes, but Converging Policies?

In view of the magnitude of global unemployment, all the customary formulas offered by economists against mass unemployment—the basic socio-economic problem of modern times—appear to be quackery. Neither quantitative, nor any kin of 'qualitative', growth will be able to eliminate the disastrous worldwide lack of jobs. For ecological reasons it is impossible to include 800 million or more unemployed in the production process through corresponding growth. The resulting increase in global Gross Domestic Product would require consumption of natural resources, energy and the environment which, given even the greatest possible productivity in those sectors, could not even be sustained for two or three decades.

In addition, aiming to achieve full employment through growth will be even more difficult even in the rich economies. For it is most likely that work productivity will continue to rise worldwide. Countries such as China, which are in the initial phase of modernisation, are still producing at a relatively still low productivity rate. But that is precisely why they can achieve notable increases in productivity in a short time by importing technology from highly-developed countries. The advantage of rapid 'catch-up rationalisation', however , is being bought at the cost of rising unemployment and progressive impoverishment.

Employment through Redistribution of Work

The notion that jobs can at some time be created for 800-900 million unemployed who will work 35 or even 40 hours a week at the productivity level of the highly-developed countries of four or five decades ago is absurd. The only realistic possibility of eliminating the world's unemployment problem is by far-reaching redistribution of work and income. The change needed for that demands fundamentally new concepts of prosperity: a reflection on the philosophy of the 'life of happiness'. 'New concepts of prosperity' means that technological progress would no longer be used mainly to deliver rising per capita incomes and excessive consumption. Instead, given a sufficient material standard of living, the quality of life would be improved primarily by shortening working hours. It is about, so to speak, assigning instrumental good sense new goals. Plus reshaping socio-economic conditions in such a way that the politicians will again be compelled to orient themselves on the good of the community and humanistic values instead of filling the pockets of the wealthy. It is sheer ideology, although very persuasive, to cite 'globalisation' and its alleged 'iron laws' in defaming the welfare state, full employment and social justice as out-of-date wishful thinking. A return to the state-guided social competitive system as practised during the first decades after the Second World War is possible just as it was politically feasible to make the transition from the old order of unfettered, ruthless capitalism to the mixed economies of the social market economy types. So it is a matter of restoring the proven structures of a mixed economic system.

However, in contrast to the first postwar decades it is now not sufficient to regenerate nation-sate interventionism. Appropriate international regualtions are required. Above all, it will depend upon reversing the new laissez-faire developments in international economic relationships which today are subsumed under the buzzword 'globalisation'. That is, to oppose over-liberalisation and its disastrous social and inhuman impacts. It will depend on the broad mobilisation of the losers in the process of globalisation whether the necessary fundamental change of course can still be made in time before a catastrophe. In particular, the new myth must be opposed that declares globalisation as a kind of law of nature and thus suggests resignation and adaptation to an allegedly unavoidable process of destruction of social and human achievements.

Mass Unemployment in the Poor Economies

The employment problems in the rich and the poor hemispheres differ not only in their magnitude, but also in their causes. The wretched condition of the poor economies is due above all to historical reasons: colonialism and, in the post-colonial era, the constraints to independent development imposed by the hegemonic influence of the rich industrial states. The waste of scarce resources by international and civil wars, and the dictatorships with their upperclass luxury consumption and inefficient, thus development obstructing exploitation structures often supported by the industrialised nations have for a long time repressed and in many cases destroyed autonomous development potential. The colonial and post-colonial distortion also contributed at least indirectly to the current population problems of the poor countries. The politically inflicted mass poverty and under-development stabilised or in fact brought about economic, socio-psychological and ideological mechanisms which oppose an effective population policy. As we know, the average educational level in many developing countries, especially among women, is too low to give a modern population policy a chance of success. Mass unemployment in the poor countries is the result of poverty. In this respect, it is about a production-side problem: to few resources, to little real and human capital, and the inefficient, unproductive use of much of the anyway limited added value of society. The picture is totally different in the rich countries the over-production economies.

Unemployment in Over-Production Systems

The main cause of mass unemployment in the industrialised nations has nothing to do with shortages. It is a phenomenon of surplus. Greater possibilities of production can no longer be used 'sufficiently profitably because the required demand is lacking. Production is done for profit. The necessary collateral condition is the satisfying of consumer needs. Employment is not even such a condition, but only a side effect which lapses immediately when labour-free production is technically possible. Thus, national income must be shared among wages and profits (or income from property). Profit is the difference between earnings and costs. Earnings depend upon demand. Macroeconomic costs consist mainly of wages and salaries (including social security contributions). These definitive connections mean that profit can be made only if overall demand is greater than the total cost labour. But in the final analysis this demand can only come from the profit-earners themselves. In his book, a Treatise on Money, Keynes described this nexus as the theory of the Widow's cruse. Under capitalistic conditions, labour is only sought or hired if profit can be earned with it. But as making a profit depends upon the demand for consumption and investment by the shareholders, it can be seen that the degree of employment is determined by the demand behaviour of the class that receives income from property. In this respect, the widespread belief that greater investment also leads to more employment, namely via the effect of investment in demand, is right.

Lower Wages Mean Lower Demand

The lower the level of wages, and given an unchanged total demand, the greater are the profits that can be made. But it is more likely that in the case of falling wages the overall demand will also drop. For stabilising total demand would require the recipients of income from property to increase their spending on consumption and/or investment to the degree to which wages and the consumption based on them fell.

During the last 10 to 15 years the development of profits in most industrialised nations has been very favourable. But profits would have grown more strongly if the demand of the shareholder had been much greater. This would have created more employment at the same time. Thus, it can be assumed that the profits are simply too high for the shareholders to be able to go in for meaningful consumption or make profitable investments. That is the reason for the extreme redirection of capital from fixed assets to portfolio investment. The growth of speculative (unproductive) financial transactions during the 1980s and 1990s (buzzword: casino capitalism), corresponded with a relatively weak formations of real capital.

Wage rises, of course, narrows the scope for profit. But precisely this effect stimulated efforts to improve the profit situation not only by investment in rationalisation, but also by investment in expansion aimed at the growing mass purchasing power. Since more is being invested, the profit mass also is growing according to the principle of the Widow's cruse. Too low wages, as it were, relieve the shareholders of the pressure to innovate and invest and allow them to earn their profits too easily. That is the real message of the 'purchasing power theory' of wages.

Over-Accumulation and Under-Consumption

Overproduction has two different causes which, however, mostly occur in tandem. They are over-investment, or creation of over-capacities, on the one hand, and lack of demand due to relative saturation and an absence of mass purchasing power on the other. But the main reason for mass unemployment in the rich hemisphere currently lies on the demand side. During the first three decades after the Second World War supply and demand rose in relative balance. Economic fluctuations showed up as temporary declines in generally positive GDP growth rates. These decades of (dynamic) balance of growth are often described today as the era of 'Fordism'. Its essential feature is that rising wages ensure continuing growth of consumption, so that equally growing profits also flow relatively continuously into investments to expand capacity and create jobs. The label 'Fordism' expresses the 'simple' view of the theory for the buying power of wages which is said to have been propagated by Henry Ford 1.This was that his workers should earn enough to be able to buy the cars they made.

The astonishingly balanced development of supply and demand from 1950 to the mid-1970s was due above all to postwar reconstruction and the pent-up demand of consumers who were starved by wartime economy shortages. This stimulated positive investment sentiment, and high investments brought at the same time high profits. The postwar growth that led within a short time to full employment was also linked with growth in productivity, which on multi-year average was more than twice that of the crisis period of the last 25 years. Thus, the so-called employment threshold (the GDP growth rate point at which employment growth begins) was much higher in those days than it is now, although there was full employment over a longer period. This simple fact opposes the thesis often propounded today that mass unemployment is above all related to rationalisation. Its is not rationalisation per se, that is, progress that boosts productivity, which is the evil. The problem is that the mistakes in distribution in supply are rooted in capitalistic structures result in increases in supply encountering insufficient demand for goods, whereby the demand for labour drops. However, the fact that demand policy contradicts the requirements of a social ethic that is ecologically responsible and right for the interests of the poor countries was already spelled out. So if a demand-oriented growth policy is practised at all, it should be designed to be as environmentally compatible as possible. After all, there are possibilities for that, such as by expanding the production of services that spares resources. A one-hour driving lesson costs more energy than one hour of ballet instruction.

The politically initiated and implemented over-liberalisation and surrender of social prosperity to global competition since the 1970s, which reproduces the old self-destructive mechanism of laissez faire, have during the last two decades markedly accelerated the crisis development inhere not in the system.

Summing Up, it is Noted that

- full employments in the rich economies would certainly be possible by means of demand policy, but only at a high cost to the environment that is concomitant with high growth rates.

- The growth policy of the rich countries impairs the poor economies' possibilities of medium to long-term growth, since these are falling back ever further in the competition for ever scarcer and thus ever more expensive resources;
- The environmental collapse currently expected for the third or fourth generation after us, which obviously also will trigger a collapse of the world economy and—probably ahead of that-armed conflicts which today are hardly imaginable, would happen very much sooner if economic growth were to be increased to such a degree that it would bring full employment worldwide;
- In the long term, the problem of global unemployment and global poverty can only be solved by a policy of massive redistribution, and in fact a redistribution of work and income, whereby increases in productivity must be used mainly or only for shortening working hours. That is a demand, which appears to be utopian. But utopias of today often have the quality of scripting the reality of tomorrow.

17

Land Tenure:

Securing Land for the Urban Poor

Around the world, especially in Asia and Africa, towns and cities are expanding rapidly. For the poorest people, finding affordable, safe and secure urban land for shelter has become increasingly difficult. This is because:

- Overall competition for land makes it increasingly costly:
- Central urban areas are being developed for commercial use;
- Natural features such as mountains or swamps limit physical urban expansion; and
- Meeting land management and planning standards (concerned with legality, technical and administrative accuracy) is expensive.
- As a result, a large and increasing proportion of urban populations are forced to live in peripheral areas or occupy marginalised and dangerous locations. These settlements are often illegal and, providing inadequate shelter and lacking essential services only exacerbate the problems of the poor. Higher levels of ill health, unemployment and non-sustainable land-use often result. Furthermore, residents may also be under constant threat of eviction by government and exploitation by landowners.

Experience shows that, if residents in such areas feel secure and safe from eviction, they do over time improve their neighbourhoods. Recognition of and granting of secure forms of tenure to previously illegal settlements often provides the incentive to communities to invest their resources in upgrading their housing and wider neighbourhoods. Security of tenure also brings the improved likelihood of basic infrastructure and other essential community services.

There is a wide range of urban land tenure systems. In many urban areas, including areas designated illegal by government, there are informal or customary tenure systems—these are often the commonest form of tenure and are expanding most rapidly.

While statutory or "legal" forms of tenure (for example freehold or leasehold agreements) offer many advantages, such as full individual rights and security and access to formal credit systems, they can also cause the very problem they were intended to solve:

- Higher rental levels, which may displace existing renters;
- The selling out of the secure land to higher income groups
- Encouragement of new illegal/informal settlements, as the poorest hope that they will also eventually get security of tenure;
- Encouragement of landowners and developers to hold land, without investing in its improvement or paying taxes on it increased value—which serves to attract even greater levels of investment and land price inflation.
- In addition, if people's incomes remain low and the capacity of the blanks or credit unions is weak, statutory forms of tenure alone may not necessarily stimulate neighbourhood improvements.

Consequently, careful analysis of existing systems of informal and customary tenure and property right is required, before embarking on major land management and tenure reforms. These can provide both acceptable levels of security and access to credit, which in turn stimulate improvements to local neighbourhoods. Before any decisions are made, tenure policies must recognise the likely impact on tenants, the poor and other vulnerable groups, especially women.

For these reasons, it is sometimes better to increase the right of residents (e.g. by protecting them from the threat of forced evictions, or by increasing their access to essential utilities or credit), rather than assuming that they need freehold or leasehold titles.

Strategies for providing shelter now recognise the diverse nature of needs, and the positive contribution which decent housing makes to social and economic development at both national and local levels. They also recognise that the most effective way of mobilising the resources required is to encourage investment in housing by individuals, communities and the private sector.

Recent experience shows that many governments are now introducing positive approaches, which are market-sensitive and encourage more efficient use of available land. These include measures to encourage landowners and developers to allocate a specified proportion of units to low-income groups out of profits generated from planning permission granted by (and therefore partly created by) the government. Public-private partnerships and revisions to planning standards and administrative procedures have also demonstrated that it is possible to reduce the costs of access to land for the poor even under conditions of market-led development, thus reducing urban sprawl, the occurrence of slum settlements and levels of poverty.

18

Democracy and Poverty:

Are they Interlinked?

Democracy assistance and poverty reduction are rightly becoming two focal and related-issues for development assistance. Increasingly, many organisations, including intergovernmental, national and civil society, are focusing their work on these two areas. Futhermore, the relationship between these two issues is complex and ever changing. There is thus a need to develop methodologies of linking democracy assistance and poverty reduction at both the policy and programme levels. International IDEA (Institute for Democracy and Electoral Assistance) in cooperation with the World Bank and the United Nations Development Programme, is developing concrete strategies that address these two objectives in a mutually reinforcing way. Through an overall situation analysis followed by regional meetings in sub-Saharan Africa, South Asia, Latin America, the Caucasus and the Arab region, the Institute has marshalled evidence of some of the key problems that affect democracy consolidation and poverty reduction in these countries:

- Corruption and its undermining effect on popular confidence in public institutions.
- Continuing economic instability coupled with the lack of strategies for addressing the twin challenges of poverty and increasing popular participation in its alleviation.
- The extremely limited nature of citizen's influence on overall policy and decision-making processes despite the spread of formal democratic institutions.

- A trend in many post-communist states towards viewing growing poverty as a direct consequence of a transition to democracy.

In short, the evidence is not very encouraging for the prospects for democracy consolidation and poverty reduction. The critical step International IDEA advocates is the development of an approach that not only seeks to put democracy as assistance and poverty reduction on top of the development assistance agenda, but also to encourage all involved to treat them as twin elements of an integrated programme of action.

Through a focus on accountable governance, promotion and protection of citizenship and rights and increased popular participation, International IDEA believes that both democracy and poverty reduction can be addressed simultaneously. Policy recommendations are being developed and will be shared in the course of this year with governments, international organisations and civil society bodies.

International IDEA believes that democracy promotion can be used as a tool for fulfilling a variety of objectives. Democracy matters because it protects human right and preserves human dignity. But democracy also matters because it helps to address some of the most critical challenges facing states today: peace, development, economic growth and stability.

Democracy does not guarantee any one of these, but increasingly it seems to be a precondition for them in the long term. Thus, advocating democracy goes beyond being a moral issue; it becomes *fundamental* to advancing the well-being of people and the stability of states. International IDEA will continue to explore the link between democracy and the major issues facing society today—and continue to argue the case for democracy.

19

Taking Poverty to Heart:

Non-Communicable Diseases and the Poor

Non-Communicable Diseases (NCDs) are the leading cause of death worldwide. Their emergence as the predominant health problem in wealthy countries accompanied economic development. As a result, NCDs are often referred to as 'diseases of affluence'. But is this a misleading term? It suggests that these are not major problems for the world's poor, which is quite simply wrong, as this article illustrates. Is it time to rethink policy on NCDs?

NCDs include cardiovascular disease (CVD), such as stroke and heart attack, diabetes, chronic lung disease, cancer, diseases of bones and joints, and mental illness. The single biggest killer is coronary heart disease, followed by other CVDs, cancer and chronic lung disease. Diabetes is a major contributor to deaths form CVD, but also causes its own unique complications. Common risk factors for these conditions include smoking, physical activity, obesity and diets high in saturated fat and sodium and low in fruit and vegetables.

By 2020, NDCs will be the biggest cause of death in all regions apart from sub-Saharan Africa. It is predicted that in 2010, the number of people with diabetes worldwide will be double the level in 1995 and that the biggest increase (both proportionately and in absolute number) will be in poorer regions. CVD occurs at an earlier age in developing countries, increasing the potential adverse economic and social consequences.

NCDs are already major health problems for adults in the poorest countries of the world. Demographic data show that age-specific death rates from NCDs in Tanzania are higher than in wealthier countries.Mortality rates for some NCDs, such as stroke, are particularly high. However, while NCDs account for 80 per cent of adult deaths in developed regions, the figure is less than 30 per cent in Tanzania, reflecting the continuing burden of infectious disease. Countries like Tanzania suffer the worst of both worlds'. Even within a country, 'diseases of affluence' is a misleading term. A more accurate label is 'diseases of urbanisation'.Several studies from developing countries show increased levels of high blood pressure and other NCD risk factors in urban compared to rural populations. Even within urban areas, the more affluent do not always suffer the greatest burden.

The rise of NCDs in developing countries is inextricably linked to economic and cultural globalisation. This is exemplified by the activities of multinational tobacco companies. Tobacco-related deaths will exceed the toll due to HIV and become the single largest preventable cause of death by 2020. Curbing the effects of globalisation on the prevention and treatment of NCDs will also require regulation of food and agriculture multinationals and the pharmaceutical and healthcare industries.

Much of the projected rise in NCDs is preventable, particularly that due to smoking, poor diet, physical inactivity and obesity. Early action in some population could prevent the emergence of these risk factors altogether; in other, the challenge is to reduce established levels. Although it is unclear whether all major risk factors are equally important in every region, the strength and consistency of data on the core risk factors in several ethnic groups justify preventative action now.

Lessons from risk factor intervention studies in rich and middle income countries suggest that success requires.

- Broad intersectoral action
- Community participation

- Appropriate legislation
- Involvement of appropriate NGOs
- Health services changes to manage those at high risk and promote public education.

Even apparently minor changes, such as a small fall in average population blood pressure, can have substantial benefits. However, some preventative pogrammes have produced disappointing results and almost all have failed to halt the ubiquitous increase in obesity. This highlights the difficulty of promoting healthy behaviour by individuals who are surrounded by barriers to change and inducements to lead an unhealthy lifestyle.

Health systems in developing countries face both a growing need for prevention programmes and increasing numbers of individuals requiring treatment. The complications of high blood pressure and diabetes can be reduced by the delivery of effective healthcare. Crucially, this entails:

- Partnership between patients and health professionals with the knowledge, ability and resources to take appropriate measures over many years.
- Cheap and effective drugs and the implementation of simple treatment protocols, as promoted by WHO and the CVD initiative of the Global Forum for Health Research.

An appropriate policy strategic framework is essential for such initiatives to be effective on a large scale. Even in the poorest countries people are already seeking healthcare for NCDs in both the public and private sectors, particularly in urban areas. Whatever the balance of priorities between different conditions, existing resources should be used as effectively as possible. Rapid evaluation methods can provide policy-makers with information on the current levels and quality of care and identify the main opportunities for improving health services.

The proper planning and co-ordination of NCD prevention and treatment, whether globally or nationally, requires up-to-date data on risk factor and disease levels—currently missing for much of the world. To address this lack, the WHO Non-Communicable Disease and Mental Health Surveillance section is promoting a standardised approach to enable comparisons across regions and over time, preparing the first ever 'world risk status' report for the major NCDs. This will provide a truly global perspective on the size and nature of the problem.

As this article has shown, NCDs are major health problems even in the world's poorest countries, including those regions where infectious diseases continue to take a huge toll. The NCD burden will grow substantially in low land middle-income countries over the next 10 to 20 years. NCDs will increasingly demand attention and require the right balance between competing priorities for prevention, cure and care. In meeting this challenge, national policy-makers will need to follow the lead of WHO and develop a strategic framework that plans for surveillance, prevention and appropriate health sector reforms.

20

Can Economic Growth Reduce Poverty?

New Findings on Inequality, Economic Growth and Poverty

Many people still think first of 'economic growth' in relation to poverty reduction. Indeed, their correlation is one of the most-discussed issues of combating poverty. The relationship is of great importance because if there is a clear causal dependency, reducing poverty could fundamentally be limited to measures to promote growth. However, if there was low growth or stagnation if would not be possible to reduce poverty decisively. In the opposite case, that of the phenomena having no causal relation, promising measures to reduce poverty could be taken up even without economic growth.

Hardly anyone now explicitly expresses the view that economic development trickles down automatically to the poor. Practical experience has refuted this assumption dating from the early days of development policy in the 1960s. However, a number of studies show development of growth and a decline in poverty running parallel. On the other hand, there are also examples which show that despite high economic growth, poverty is not reduced markedly. The common answer to the question this raises is thus: Yes, growth can reduce poverty, but only if additional measures oriented on the poor are taken up. This is often termed pro-poor-growth. But what that means in detail, and whether economic growth as such plays a causal role at all, is not clarified. It is worth taking a look at the arguments on the basis of more recent empirical and theoretical knowledge.

No Direct Causality Between Growth and Poverty Reduction

Among the many indicators of poverty, the income of the poor (income poverty) has the closest relationship to economic growth. An increase in gross domestic product and thus national income could, if other factors come into play be linked with an increase in the per capita income of the poor.

Such a relationship between economic growth and the income of the poor, however, cannot be described as causal, as is asserted implicitly time and again by the statements that growth is a necessary but not sufficient precondition for poverty reduction. In so far as growth and poverty reduction arise at the same time at the end of a process, they exist alongside each other. It would be almost a tautology to say that the former is the cause or part-cause of the latter. Both express the same thing, namely a change in per capita income as well, and both have similar causes. What matters is recognising what these causes are and what specific factors must come into play so that the income of the poor grows too. Growth as a "prerequisite" or "condition" is then no longer the focus; the priority is asking for specific policies that result in higher incomes for the poor. The detour in thinking about growth is not necessary. Since, however, it is based on similar factors, such as fiscal policy/budget structure, employment policy, combating inflation, and institutional development, economic growth can also emerge if poverty is reduced. The difference of views lies in the fact that under the heading 'poverty reduction' the aim is no longer growth, but a purposeful reduction of poverty.

Therefore, in reverse, successful combating of poverty can be seen as being the cause of growth insofar as activating the capabilities of the poor and using their productive capacity of the poor and using their productive capacity triggers economic drive.

Indirect Causality Between Growth and Poverty Reduction?

So even if economic growth fundamentally has no direct causal impact on poverty, growth still can reduce it indirectly. This is the case when due to positive economic development a government has greater revenue and uses the surplus for combating poverty, for example by providing such public goods as education and health services. Also in these cases, however, growth is not a compelling precondition. Even without growth greater government revenue can be achieved for example by more efficient tax collection. And leeway for social welfare spending can be gained by redistributing the budget, such as by cutting military appropriations. Furthermore, an automatic process is not given because the government can also use surplus funds for non-social purposes.

Creation of jobs due to increased economic activity can be another indirect link between economic growth and income poverty, if such a development generates income and reduces poverty. But also in this case I see no compelling causality because, for instance, industrial jobs are not necessarily open to the really poor. In addition, these positive impacts occur to a considerable extent only in the event of labour-intensive development. In many countries, however, economic growth is achieved by capital-intensive production.

Inequality, Growth and Income Poverty

If national incomes, grow, a naïve observer might assume that the income of the poor must also grow along with it. But that would be a statistical fallacy. Even if only the income of the rich grows, this results in macroeconomics statistics showing a higher per capita income. What the true conditions are is shown as soon as one divides the population statistically into income groups, such as in fifths, as is usual. It then turns out that the bald figures on average per capital growth can certainly cloak a situation where the income of the richest fifth of the population is growing fast while that of the poorest fifth is stagnating. Despite growth, the gap between the two becomes even wider.

The unequal distribution of income (and of other assets such as property and access to social services), and its connection to poverty reduction and growth has recently returned to the forefront of the debate.

It is obvious that inequality and its changes have direct effects on the poverty situation. Does inequality also have an impact on poverty via its relation to growth, because growth promotes or reduces inequality? Earlier, the predominant view was that rapid growth was linked with atleast a temporary increase in inequality, so that a distinct policy of growth initially disadvantaged the poor.

The current dominant view is that growth has no foreseeable effects on inequality and that inequality changes only very slowly, in reverse, however, it is assumed that greater equality is a determinant of growth. According to that view, an indirect relationship between poverty on one side and inequality as a factor dependent upon growth on the other is not given.

That leads to the conclusion that fair distribution has more weight than growth. Fair distribution, however, does not depend upon growth. An appropriate policy is possible at any time, not only after an economic situation has improved. The notion that still shimmers through the debate that "something must be earned first before it can be distributed", is wrong. It is a matter of designing policy and the entire economic process right from the start in such a way that the surplus benefits all including the poor. Important elements of such a policy are, for example, land reform and development of finance systems.

Relationship of Growth to Poverty

According to today's conventional wisdom, income poverty expresses only a part of what poverty means. Not least through the voices of the poor themselves, it has become clear that violation of human dignity and rights, a lack of participation in decisions and exclusion from society, unequal treatment of men and women, and vulnerability are also regarded as poverty. For poverty is caused to a great degree by conflicts of power and interests. Income poverty often is not even seen as the greatest problem.

What relationship do these more far reaching characteristics of poverty have to economic growth? A direct relationship of growth to socially-related aspects such as women's inheritance rights, land rights and exclusion from decisions cannot be seen. Considerable improvements in favour of the poor can be achieved here even without economic growth.

Those who see a strong and causal connection between economic growth and poverty reduction must ask themselves what the prospects are for high growth rates and thus for a decline in poverty. Coupling poverty reduction to economic growth is problematic. If only low growth rates are to be expected.

Another question is whether continuous increases in growth are at all desirable and possible in the medium to long term. In this connection, a difference should perhaps be made between developing countries and industrialised nations. But environmental compatibility and availability of resources set limits to growth for both. Some academics assume that industrialised nations have already reached an inherent limit (stagnation theory) and that the high growth rates of earlier years will not return. Moreover, they add, full employment is no longer achievable due to, among other things, an ongoing increase in productivity, and current unemployment cannot be reduced by customary means. In any case, if growth were to be taken as the major benchmark, the prospects for a radical reduction of income poverty around the world would be modest.

Summing Up

Poverty is a complex problem and reducing it depends upon many interconnected factors that is why poverty cannot be attributed to one main cause nor its reduction based on one main strategy. Economic growth is just one strategic element among many others related to poverty reduction. An indirect causal connection between growth and poverty reduction can only be seen because governments will have a greater scope for action due to economic growth, and if they promote labour-intensive development.

Therefore growth's role in poverty reduction must be put into perspective growth cannot be the first thing that comes to mind, nor is it the golden path to reducing poverty. The simplistic theory of economic growth as the main condition obstructs the bigger picture; it clings to the underlying and ongoing belief in the trickle-down effect. Even if there is no growth or for inherent reasons there can be none, there are promising ways to take on the challenge of mass poverty in the developing countries. Up front, governments and bilateral and multilateral donors must have the political will to design economic, financial and social policies so that they are oriented on poverty in a coherent way—the result can also be economic growth.

21

Pro-Poor Tourism:

Opportunities for Sustainable Local Development

Tourism is the world's largest industry, with over 10 per cent of GDP globally directly related to tourism activities. Rising standards of living in the countries of the North, declining long-haul travel costs, increasing holiday entitlements, changing demographics and strong consumer demand for exotic international travel have resulted in significant tourism growth to developing countries. Tourism is the principal export for one third of developing countries. Tourism brings relatively powerful consumers to Southern countries, potentially an important market for local entrepreneurs and an engine for local sustainable economic development. There is no reliable data on domestic tourism but it is growing rapidly in South America and in China and South East Asia; it represents a very significant economic opportunity for many local communities.

Tourism and Aid

Multilateral and bilateral aid agencies are wary of involving themselves in the tourism sector. In 1969 the World Bank created a Tourism Projects Department recognising that in the Mediterranean and Adriatic countries, and in Mexico, tourism had been a significant generator of foreign exchange and of direct and indirect employment, internationally in the late nineteen sixties, there was considerable concern about high rates of unemployment and the ability of developing countries to service debt. Tourism sector studies were completed in some 31 countries and tourism staff regularly participated in World Bank macro-economic missions—their reports focussed on the potential for growth in tax revenues, foreign exchange earnings and direct and indirect employment effects. The primary emphasis was on national economic impact. By 1978 when the World Bank closed its Tourism Projects Department of the Bank had provided loans and credits for 18 projects in 14 countries and it was the major source of funds and technical assistance for tourism development. The bank withdrew from tourism development for a range of reasons amongst which were anxieties about the role of the bank in funding projects to develop luxury hotels designed to attract wealthy travellers from the developed countries. This strategy was seen inconsistent with new policy objectives which prioritised the bottom 40 per cent, the Bank's priorities were shifting towards the poor, a group, which was gaining relatively little from tourism development. There was a growing literature that focussed on the negative economic, social and cultural impacts of unmanaged tourism on local communities. The fuel crises of the nineteen seventies also undermined some of the forecasts that had been made for the strength of the market and the Bank withdrew from the sector in parallel with most other multilateral and bilateral agencies.

The international agencies followed a macro-economic tourism agenda in the nineteen seventies and eighties focusing on tax and foreign exchange revenues at the national level, major hotel and resort development, international promotion and national and regional master planning all attracted funding. In the nineties the adoption of the new poverty elimination target of halving the number of people living on less than 1 US $ per day by 2015 refocussed development assistance on pro-poor growth. Multilateral and bilateral aid agency agendas are shifting towards micro economic strategies, which benefit local communities and in particular those below the poverty threshold. With poverty elimination now at the heart of decision aid, the potential for using tourism to generate pro-poor economic growth is being reassessed.

Since the mid-1980s, interest in 'green' tourism, eco-tourism and community tourism has grown rapidly among tour operators, policy makers, advocates and researchers. All of these focus on the need to ensure that tourism does not erode the environmental and cultural base on which it depends. The emphasis has been on minimising social, cultural and environmental impacts; rather than on positively affecting the livelihoods of the poor.

The Potential of Pro-Poor Tourism

There are a number of reasons to look again at tourism and to assess its potential to generate pro-poor growth, 80 per cent of the world's poor live in just 12 countries and tourism is significant or growing in all but one of them. Tourism is a very large sector, it is growing rapidly, and there is some evidence that it is relatively labour intensive. The consumer travels to the destination, creating additional—local—opportunities for the sale of additional goods and services—ranging from local pottery to a guided walk. Tourism can be used to diversify local economies; it can often be developed in remote and marginal areas with few other diversifications or export opportunities. These areas often attract tourists because of their high landscape, cultural and wildlife values. These natural resources and the local culture are amongst the few assets of the poor.

Pro-poor tourism generates net benefits for the poor. It can be defined as forms of tourism where the benefits to the poor are greater than costs which tourism brings them. Economic costs and benefits are clearly imported but social environmental and cultural costs and benefits are clearly important, but social and benefits also need to be taken into account. Pro poor tourism aims to expand opportunities for those living on less than 1US$ per day. Whilst it will also need to be sustainable preserving local culture, minimizing environmental impacts, it will be driven by the poverty agenda. Community-based tourism seeks to promote initiatives by local communities or individuals within them; much has been learnt from these projects. Maximizing the poverty elimination effect requires that the emphasis is placed on involving those people who are living on less than 1 US$ per day and creating economic opportunities for them. Not all community tourism is pro-poor in this sense.

Effects on the Livelihoods of the Poor

Assessing the livelihood impacts of tourism is not simply a matter of counting jobs or wage income. Participatory poverty assessments demonstrate great variety in the priorities of the poor and factors affecting livelihood security and sustainability. Tourism can affect many of these, positively and negatively, often indirectly. It is important to assess these impacts and their distribution.

Tourism can generate four different types of local cash income generally involving different categories of people:

- wages from formal employment;
- earnings from selling goods, services, or casual labour (e.g., food, crafts, building materials, guide services);
- and profits arising from locally owned enterprises
- Income: this may include profits from a community run enterprise, dividends from a private sector partnership and land rental paid by an investor.

Waged employment can be sufficient to lift a household from insecure to secure. But it may only be an available to a minority, and not to the poor. Casual earnings per person may be very small, but much more widely spread and may be enough, for instance, to cover school fees for one or more children. Work as a tourist guide although casual, is often of high status and relatively well paid. There are relatively few examples of successful and sustainable collective income from tourism.

Negative economic impacts include inflation, dominance by outsiders in land markets and in-migration, which erodes economic opportunities for the local poor. Impacts differ between men and women. Women can be the first to suffer from loss of natural resources (e.g., access to fuel wood) and cultural/sexual exploitation, but may benefit most from physical infrastructure improvements (e.g. piped water or a grinding mill) where this is a by product of tourism.

Positive Development Impacts of Tourism

On the positive side, tourism can generate funds for investments in health, education and other assets, provide infrastructure, stimulate development of social capital, strengthen sustainable management of natural resources, and create a demand for improved assets (especially education). On the negative side, tourism can reduce local access to natural resources draw heavily upon local infrastructure, and disrupt social networks.

Tourism affects the livelihoods of the poor by changing their access to assets. In several cases, tourism's impact on people's access to natural resources or physical infrastructure has been identified as the most important benefit or concern.

Cultural Impacts of Tourism can be Positive or Negative

Local residents often highlight the way tourism affects other livelihood goals whether positively or negatively—such as cultural pride, a sense of control, good health, and reduced vulnerability. Socio-cultural intrusion by tourists is often cited as a negative impact. Certainly sexual exploitation particularly affects the poorest women, girls and young men. The poor themselves may view other types of cultural change as positive. Tourism can also increase the value attributed to minority cultures by national policy-makers. Overall, the cultural impacts of tourism are hard to disentangle from wider processes of development.

The overall balance of positive and negative livelihood impacts will vary enormously between situations, among people and over time, and particularly in the extent to which local priorities are able to influence the planning process. The application of a 'sustainable' livelihood framework is essential to developing pro-poor approaches. The distribution of livelihood impacts has to be considered. The poor are far from being a homogenous group. The positive and negative impacts of tourism will inevitably be distributed unevenly among poor groups, reflecting different patterns of assets, activities, opportunities and choices. The most substantial benefits, particularly jobs, may be concentrated among few. Net benefits are likely to be smallest, or negative, for the poorest.

Policies to Enhance Pro-Poor Tourism

Despite innumerable case studies of tourism development, there is relatively little assessment of practical experience in strategies to make tourism more pro-poor. Nevertheless, lessons can be drawn from a wealth of small initiatives (many from 'community tourism' or 'conservation and development' programmes), supplemented by expanding knowledge on 'pro-poor growth strategies', several policy implications clearly emerge.

1. *Put Poverty Issues on the Tourism Agenda*

A first step is to recognise that enhancing the poverty impacts of tourism is different from commercial, environmental or ethical concerns. PPT can be incorporated as an additional objective, but this requires pro-active and strategic intervention. There may well be trade-offs to make- for example between attracting all-inclusive operators and maximising informal sector opportunities, or between faster growth through outside investment, and slower growth building on local capacity. These trade-offs need to be addressed.

2. *Enhance Economic Opportunities and a Wide Range of Impacts*

Two approaches need to be combined:

- Expand poor people's economic participation by addressing the barriers they face, and maximising a wide range of employment, self-employment and informal sector opportunities;
- Incorporate wider concerns of the poor into decision-making. Reducing competition for natural resources, minimising trade-offs with other livelihood activities,

using tourism to create physical infrastructure that benefits the poor and addressing cultural disruption will often be particularly important.

3. *A Multi-level Approach*

Pro-poor interventions can and should be taken at three different levels:

- this is where pro-active practical partnerships can be developed between operators, residents, NGOs and local authorities, to maximise benefits;
- national policy level-policy reform may be needed on a range of tourism issues (planning, licensing, training) and non-tourism issues (land tenure, business incentives, infrastructure, land-use planning);
- International level—to encourage responsible consumer and business behaviour, and to enhance commercial codes of conduct.

4. *Work Through Partnerships, Including Business and Tourists*

National and local governments, private enterprises, industry associations, NGOs, community organisations, consumers, and donors all have a role to play. It is particularly important to engage business, and to ensure that initiatives are commercially realistic and integrated into main stream operations. Private operators will not be able to devote substantial time and resources to developing pro-poor actions. NGOs and donors can help in reducing the transaction costs of changing commercial practice—for example facilitating the training, organisation, and communication that would enable businesses to use more local suppliers. Changing the attitudes of tourists (at both international and national levels) is also essential if pro-poor tourism is to be commercially viable and sustainable.

5. *Incorporate pro-poor tourism approaches into mainstream tourism*

Pro-poor tourism should not just be pursued in niche marchets (such as eco-tourism or community tourism). It is even more important that mass tourism is developed in ways that benefit the poor. It is also important to assess which tourism segments are particularly relevant to poor. Domestic tourists are likely to be important customers.

6. *Reform Decision-Making Systems*

It is impossible to prescribe exactly how each tourism enterprise should develop in ways that best fit with livelihoods. The most important principle is to enhance the participation of the poor. Three different ways of doing this can be identified:

- Strengthen rights at local level (e.g., tenure over tourism assets), so that local people have market power and make their own decisions over developments.
- Develop more participatory planning.
- Use planning gain and other incentives to encourage private investors to enhance local benefits. These approaches require implementation capacity among governmental and non-governmental institutions within the destination, and require a supportive national policy framework.

It is time to reconsider the role of tourism in contributing to pro-poor development. Tourism should be judged against other possible strategies and where it offers the best opportunities for pro-poor growth, or where it can make a useful contribution by increasing the diversity of opportunities for the poor, tourism it should be considered. However, careful and effective local management will be essential if it is to contribute to meeting poverty targets and if tourism dependency is to be avoided.

22

Heating up Environmental Education and Communication

Worldwide environmental issues ranging from the hazardous waste in your backyard to ozone depletion far away in the atmosphere can threaten our planet and compromise our quality of life. The positive and negative effects of environmental interactions are just beginning to be better understood and addressed. Within this context, environmental education and communication have a remarkable opportunity to accelerate understanding and to mobilize national and community participation in change.

Communication because it is the exchange of information. In social programmes, its effectiveness depends on assessing audience needs and taking into account the social, cultural and economic aspects of problem as well as the quality of education messages and materials.

Education because it involves learning—learning how to think about an issue and its solution; how to acquire and refine skills for solving problems; how to transfer what is learned from situation to situation.

In social programmes, communication and education together lead to increased public participation in problem-solving and in activities which promote change. The participation of many individuals over time can lead to changed expectations for individual behaviour and institutional practices.

The process of communication and education together might be thought of as the "heating up" of a society around an issue through the "saturation" of all available channels of communication. In a "hot" society, all channels of communication and the processes of individual and social change reinforce a message. From the perspective of designing an education and communication programme, this might be called the "saturation" approach to social change.

Example of 'Saturation'

A decade ago, research information about the link between smoking and chronic disease, particularly cancer and heart attack, was communicated to health professionals in a hostile environment where smoking was considered socially "in". But information campaigns by governments and cancer/heart associations put smoking on the public agenda. The result? Conversations about smoking increased within households, doctors' offices and in laboratories. Community organisations began to take action. Schools and the work place joined in.

No-smoking campaigns became a catalyst for change in attitudes and behaviour in health with "smoking" as a unifying symbol. Under the umbrella of "smoking", the rituals and behaviours associated with smoking were individually affected by the saturation process. Therefore other health activities related to smoking also reaped the benefits. Extending the impact of saturation can be applied to other contexts.

Today, a new global image is emerging—an image which represents the environment and unifies people behind its common cause. The symbol of a "Green" earth and the colour "green" are perpetuating an environmental movement, the result of and an inspiration to environmental education and communication efforts everywhere.

"Green" political parties are gaining popular support. All over the world "green" label marketing approaches are influencing consumer behaviour. Just as in the smoking example, acting upon the unifying symbol of "green" through environmental education and communication has the potential to strengthen programmes and further heat up public consciousness. Environmental education and communication provides the opportunity to support policy change, institutional change and behaviour change in highly segmented audiences.

Stage 1: Setting the Public Agenda

Globally, the public is already talking about the environment. Numerous single-issue environmental groups and educational programmes are already in operation. People become ready to talk about, think about and support environmental activities. Membership in existing environmental groups increases, and new programmes and opportunities for popular participation appear.

Stage 2: Engaging Key Institutions

Building alliances and collaboration among institutions creates a network. Lead institutions reach out to other institutions representing social process—education, work, religion and government—and initiate collaborative educational activities. For example, school systems integrate environmental modules within existing curricula and initiate teacher training and youth ecoclubs. Community based action increasingly addresses local issues such as garbage collection and industrial pollutants. Media coverage responds more frequently and positively.

Stage 3: Establishing a New Environmental Order

Governmental and non-governmental institutions become the initiators of environmental education, and participation becomes broader and more diverse. Specific target audiences begin to modify their role with regard to particular environmental problems. Community mobilisation increasingly generates demand for appropriate regulatory change. Expectations for appropriate individual and social behaviour begin to change. Finally, "Green" positions become "in", "non-Green" positions "out".

Applied Research

Experience with development communication in other

sectors leads to optimism in reaching new levels of excellence in combining environmental education and communication. Perhaps the most important element in "putting it all together", however, is to maintain commitment to well-tried applied research procedures.

- Investigation of target audience characteristics (including socio-economic, gender and cultural) and attributes (attitudinal and behavioural) in relation to local environmental issues provides insight into an appropriate model of behaviour change and effective educational strategies, messages and materials.
- Limited testing of innovative strategies devised for local situations will uncover refinements needed for broader application.
- Comparison studies between the impact of different educational strategies with similar objectives will provide a basis for future strategic choices.
- Standardized indicators of impact and evaluation studies will provide an assessment of the progress and impact of programmes and, to some extent, the relative power of different components within the programmes.
- Content analyses of mass media over time will provide profiles of societies "heating up" on environmental issues.
- Description of the differences between industrialized country and developing country objectives, programme content and impact will provide a source of new insight about the process of social and individual change.

In addition, applied research can also advance the state of the art for environmental education and communication when properly field tested. There are two major sources for such innovation:

1. the refinement of social change theory at universities and research firms;

2. "creative" concepts with proved efficacy in other sectors such as the "enter-educate" approach (education through entertainment) in the population sector.

This description of the potential and progress of environmental education and communication is, in reality, a call to action. The "heating up" of societies on environmental issues is technically within our reach through environmental education and communication programmes. It is up to us to develop the funding, the research-based strategies—and the communication among professionals about results, both successes and failure—required to make it happen.

23

Economics and Environment

Statistics change our view of the world. So statistics, however objective and accurate, are never value free but focus on what societies deem important. For better or worse, they guide government, business and individual decisions.

Until recently, the old game of India's economic growth was unquestioned and the score was kept between the national players by comparing their Gross National Product (GNP) or its narrower domestic version, Gross Domestic Product (GDP). It is time to take a closer look at the proliferation of new scoreboards, statistics and quality-of-life indexes which will redefine wealth and progress and change the future direction of human society.

Clarifying Values

These new scorecards and the 'greening' of GNP/GDP national accounts reflect the new 'green' accounting in thousands of balance sheets, reports and books on environment. At the very least, assumptions underlying old and new indicators are being clarified. The debate is still over what rather than how to measure, and what to do about values and amenities that are priceless.

The costs of GNP growth are now obvious—from felled forests, pollution exhausted soils, depleted natural resources and holes in the ozone layer to disrupted cultures and communities.

The concept of GNP/GDP was adapted into national accounting in India. With little re-examination, it continues to value bombs and bullets (defence expenditure), highly while setting the values of defence expenditure, education and public infrastructure—not to mention clean air and water and other environmental assets—at zero. It also ignores the some 50 per cent of production, which it unpaid—such as do-it-yourself home construction and repairs, food growing, household maintenance, parenting children and volunteering. In India such unpaid work can comprise up to 75 per cent of all production, particularly in agriculture sector.

Systems of National Accounts are based on GNP/GDP. Few economists, trade negotiators or development agencies questioned the basic assumption underlying it: that economies were generally in equilibrium, and that adding up a society's production and exchange of goods and services, measured in money terms, defined wealth and progress—however many social and environmental 'bads' came along with the 'goods'. Today's debates concern how best to calculate the costs of these 'bads' of production passed on to taxpayers or future generations. Some are easy to quantify: Costs of cleaning up pollution can be calculated, and their increase marches in lock-step with the expansion of pollution control and environment industry sectors.

Confusing means with ends: Indian Government officials, business executives, academics and hundreds of thousands of civic organisations are beginning to agree that we have been confusing means (i.e. GNP growth) with ends (human development and the survival and further evolution of our species under drastically changed planetary conditions).

New environmental and resource realities, legislation and insurance liabilities are driving further overhauling of traditional accounts. There is a big issue over whether new indicators will be weighted in money terms to expand GDP, or whether the separate components—health, education, environment, etc. - should be 'unbundled' so that the public can follow their own concern and hold politicians accountable for results:

Macroeconomists still try to expand GDP by pricing environmental amenities and costs. Social and natural scientists, while agreeing that environmental amenities must be valued at more than zero in GDP, advocate 'unbundled' physical indicators, such as water and air quality measure and rates of infant mortality. They suspect that economists 'contingent prices' for valuing the environment are theoretical and arbitrary.

Such 'Shadow prices' are derived by economists from historic welfare theories and formulas based on 'willingness to pay' (WTP) of willingness to be compensated'. Thus, to arrive at a price for valuing a marshland (one of the most productive ecosystem on the planet), economists could poll voters and residents with no motives other than appreciation for marshes and their non-monetary or aesthetic values or their desire to preserve them and the rare species they might contain. Such contingent prices would be lower than those offered by a hotel developer with profit motives or by a biotechnology firm which had identified species in the area that could be used for pharmaceutical products. Worse, such pricing discounts poor people's needs and concerns, since they cannot afford to participate. Here the price system should be subordinated to more democratic decision-making, such as voting on whether or not to protect the marsh.

Economic Accountability

Most social and natural scientists, as well as voters, believe that economics must now take its place within interdisciplinary teams of statisticians from health, education, energy and environmental policy fields. Economics is not a science by rigorous standards, but a profession often lacking in the quality assurances and accountability that governs lawyers and doctors. GNP is a malfunctioning strand of our 'cultural DNA code' - carrying erroneous information and signalling to the body - politic a form of growth analogous to that of cancer cells which consume the host's body. The new national accounting methods being redesigned to correct or even replace GNP/GDP will function like healthy' cultural DNA strands', newly spliced in to govern healthier growth and more normal development patterns for human societies. Quantitative growth is dominant as children grow to adulthood, but once their mature size and weight are reached, this gives way to qualitative growth: education, social skills, broader awareness and even greater ethical understanding and wisdom. The statistical shift from GNP/GDP to sustainable development indicators mirrors such maturing of societies, recognising new goals and the traits human beings must now rapidly develop if we are to restructure our society for sustainability.

The new scorecards allow Indians to move beyond economism and ideologies of left and right to measure results directly and hold our business and government leaders accountable for implementing progress on the major goals of individual voters, consumers and investors. The new scorecards can help broaden trade pacts to include sustainable development criteria.

24

Tourism and the Environment

The relationship between tourism and the environment is obvious, and is largely established through what is sometimes called "environment quality". This quality is perceived in different ways according to the human population and the circumstances presiding tourist activities at any given moment. Any analysis of the relationship between tourism and the environment that we can include under human ecology therefore comprises aspects of the natural sciences as well as the social sciences.

Tourist activity is promoted, conditioned and influenced by the environmental circumstances of each region and can be affected by modifications or changes in those circumstances. Although a lot of emphasis has been placed on the negative impact or modifications in "environment quality" attributed to tourism, it is also accepted that it can be a very important factor in the preservation and defence of ecological values threatened by more destructive alternative for the use of territory. Very often, tourism can be the most suitable and most satisfactory way of using a region's renewable natural resources. Nevertheless, their management and use need to be properly regulated so as to guarantee their renewability and persistence.

There is room in this complex field of relations to study, rationalize and optimize an activity as important as tourism, form the point of view of its insertion in the ecological systems with which it interacts. However, there are relatively few efficient studies on issues of real importance. It is startling to observe that places with tourist potential undertake little or no research in this field.

One possible cause is the difficulty in identifying the real problematic in tourism/environment relations, which is essentially interdisciplinary and involves the integration of traditionally separate areas of knowledge. Although work is undertaken from time to time on environmental psychology, the sociology of tourism, behaviour in relation to the environment, etc., they are very rarely combined with works on the environment, forestry and agricultural policies, soil use, contamination, biodiversity, evaluation of environmental impact, nature conservation, etc., in search for a more integrated management of tourist resources.

Responsible Tourism

Tourism runs the risk of going the way of other phenomena, which first of all experience rapid growth and then suffer a spectacular collapse, what in Economics is often called "boom and bust"

The causes are familiar: a certain dose of greed, often based on a lack of mid or long-term planning, property speculation, little consideration for local populations—in both economic and social aspects—and, in general, a lack of awareness as regards environmental aspects—contamination, water use, energy, etc., on the part of tour operators, hoteliers and other agents involved in tourism in its different forms, including the tourists themselves. The problem is particularly evident in ecotourism, based on the wonders of he natural world: landscapes, flora and fauna. Many experts fear for the future of this type of tourism, which has grown spectacularly in the last few years. Landscapes deteriorate, the fauna decreases, the designers and administrators of tourist developments fail to respect the most elementary principles for adapting architecture to its surroundings, or else there is little effort to recycle, economize or educate with a few honourable exceptions, tourist planning is careless and irresponsible.

And yet a responsible approach would be in the tour operators' own interests, as it would make the tourist industry sustainable, with positive influences on biological, economic and social aspects.

Ecotourism, for example, has shown that when properly conceived it can become a powerful instrument for the preservation of nature, with very favourable repercussions for local populations and for educational programmes, while offering hundreds of millions of ecotourists a wide range of spiritual and physical satisfactions. At the same time, the host countries can take pride in what they have to offer their citizens and the rest of the world.

The preventive and corrective measures are known to us; what is needed is a sense of responsibility and farsightedness on the part both of the authorities and of the industry. We need regulations and controls, so as to put the people who do the damage out of circulation an reward those at the forefront of sustainability

Sustainable Tourism

After several decades of rapid quantitative growth, tourism is going through a period of profound transformation. Tourists, the consumer in this industry, but also the public, have started to demand a change in the conditions of production and use of tourist service, putting an end to the uncontrolled expansion of mass tourism.

This is the ultimate reason, apart from ethical and aesthetic considerations, why tourist activity as a whole, in the private sector as well as in the public and voluntary (NGO) sector, has begun to seriously analyse the implications of tourism in terms of socio-cultural and environmental impacts, and to consider the need to draw up and implement environment friendly tourist policies.

Indeed, while not denying the viability and the utility of alternative approaches of an external and coercive nature, it is obvious that the decision-maker in the sector react better to positive stimuli. The realisation that their clients prefer well-conserved areas and non-aggressive tourist practices and that they are prepared to pay more for this makes it easier to adopt strategies of sustainability in the tourist industry in a sincere alliance with conservation movements.

All this points to the validity of Overall Quality Management as a viable method in sustainable tourist activities. The overall quality approach renders the management of products and especially of tourist areas extremely sensitive to the preferences and expectations of consumers. The private public profitability of a tourist destination will depend on clients' satisfaction, since these will return more often and for longer and will pass on a positive image of their holiday experiences. In so far as these preferences and expectations include the demand for unspoilt settings, consumer satisfaction, and therefore the profitability of a tourist spot, will call for the development of strategies for sustainable development.

One can believe this is a productive approach for sustainability in the tourist business and one that makes for professional attitudes that fit in with the economic targets of businesses and other organisations. There is only one prior requirement: continued education and training of everyone involved in tourism, from consumers to those responsible for tourist policies. The demand for quality, and even more so for environmental quality, is a call to people's awareness, to their understanding of the environmental and cultural implications of any activity and their ability to express themselves and to organize to choose the most clear-sighted line of action.

Tourism in the Modern Age

What will the tourist trade of the year 2000 be like? Who will be the tourists of the coming millennium? These are the questions which, faced with the extraordinary boom in tourism, experts, tour operators and politicians have repeatedly posed over the last fifteen years. These questions arise either because of the financial profits the tourist industry involves, or from the demands of consumers who show new awarenesses, habits and lifestyles. In the eighties, mass tourism gradually changed and people began to talk of "tourisms". Expressions such as cultural tourism, sports tourism, religious tourism, adventure tourism or ecotourism have become part of everyday language. In the past the dominant practices was to take one long holiday in a single destination, today, people tend to distribute their holidays over different destinations and different times of the year.

From a socio-historical point of view, three types of tourist industry can be differentiated. In the case of the industrial tourist, for whom work is the center of existence, the motivations for travelling can be summed up as rest and freedom from responsibilities. This type is gradually decreasing in number. The hedonistic tourist belongs to the generation that discovered entertainment and consumerism. They like to go on holiday to experiment, to explore the unknown, enjoy themselves, meet other people and relax in unspoilt natural surroundings. These are the majority today and will continue to be so. Finally, the modern age tourist, someone who tends to reduce the polarity between work and play: not just work, but just not fun, either. Their reasons for travelling include broadening their personal horizons and getting back to simple things and nature, with a touch of creativity in the planning of their journey. These are gradually growing in number and in future will form an important segment of demand.

One characteristic in the expectations of the modern age tourist is the capacity to make a critical appraisal of the offer and to influence it. Producers should be more attentive and sensitive to the new demands and be flexible enough to cater for the tourist in search of higher quality. In the third millennium in fact, the concept of quality will have to take environmental aspects more into account. Recent forms of tourism point to a renewed interest in nature and a wish for quality tourism. So much so, that some tourist spots are reorganising their own offer in keeping with these trends. Quality is the result of a complex strategy which is organised day by day. The consumers, whose environmental awareness is constantly growing, will expect to identify, verify and be able to differentiate ecologically correct products from the imitations now invading the market.

The present millennium is coming to an end and is leaving Western countries with a high level of welfare and a large tourist demand to satisfy. Nevertheless, serious environmental problems also plague areas that receive a high influx of tourists. Tourists, tour operators, local authorities and the general public are therefore called on to find new forms of coexistence and the right solutions for themselves and for the survival of the planet.

25

Fresh Water and the Environment

It is widely recognized that water is going to be one of the major issues confronting humanity at the turn of the century and beyond. We are facing a crisis as regards the quantity and quality of water supply, but we have yet to experience full social and political impact of that crisis. The escalation in the population and the quest for continued development is leading to conflicting pressures on water resources. Such resources are the ultimate recipient of pollution from various socio-economic activities associated with urbanisation, agriculture, mining and clearing of native vegetation. Pollution originating from human waste, especially where appropriate sanitation facilities are not available, or are located too close to water supply sources affects both surface water and ground water.

This makes water supply and health perhaps the most important issue for the large proportion of the global population. Paradoxically, the demands for "sustainable management" and increasing global population require more potable water from a declining available potable water base.

It is universally accepted that proper water administration is a critical component of sustainable development—that is, development that meets the needs of both present and future generations. Indeed, water is an essential factor in a large number of productive activities, of which one of the most important is the production of food by irrigation. This activity, accounts for two thirds of the water resources used by humanity. A supply of drinking water and sanitation in urban centres are crucial for preserving human health.

For some decades it has been known that the misuse of water resources is responsible for many important environment problems. For example, in many industrialized cities both surface water and ground water are seriously contaminated. This deterioration is a consequence of a range of human activities, sometimes in isolation, others over a large area or a long period of time. Among examples of the latter is modern agriculture, whether it uses irrigation or not, as a result of the intensive use made of mineral fertilizers and pesticides.

Water Shortage: Exaggeration, Reality or Bad Management?

Some of these problems have made news and have created the impression the water shortage will be one of humanity's big problems in the coming decades. Sometimes this feeling is due to genuinely manipulative publicity campaigns to justify the setting in motion of hydraulic megaprojects which basically benefit a few large construction companies. The truth is that except for a handful of very specific cases, no problems of water shortage are to be found almost anywhere. On the other hand, cases of bad water management are not rare at all.

Basic Principles for Good Water Management

Good management of water resources—and of almost all other natural resources—must be based on the principles of solidarity, "subsidiarity" and participation. The physical reality requires that these resources be considered a common heritage of humanity both now and in the future. By "subsidiarity" we mean that water management should be as decentralized as possible: what one person or any minor social group can do should not be done by a higher authority. For example, what local government can do should not be done a regional, state or central government. Participation consists in water users playing as large a part as possible in decisions affecting water, in keeping with each state's or country's social and cultural structure. Obviously this participation calls for a certain cultural and technical knowledge—a hydrological education—on the part of those users.

The need for participation by users is even greater in the exploitation of groundwater. In this case, users tend to extract water independently of one another. They often fail to realize, until there is a serious economic or environmental impact, that their pumping affects other people who rely on the same water supply as has happened.

Water shortage is rarely a serious problem: in fact, in some cases the problem is exaggerated to justify the construction of large works using taxpayer's money. On the other hand, the contamination of surface and groundwater tends to be a problem which rarely receives adequate treatment. Successful water management should be based on three basic principles: solidarity, subsidiarity and participation. The specific way in which these principles are applied will vary from one state or country to another, but the effectiveness of water management will depend in large measure on the hydrological education of the general public.

The universal way of obtaining freshwater is from rain. River systems are the results of the excess water that falls on dry land in the form of rain. On the one hand, rainwater penetrates the permeable soils, saturates them and accumulates to form groundwater reservoirs, or aquifers, which can come to the surface in the form of springs. On the other hand, the water is absorbed by vegetation, which uses it for pumping minerals and then evaporates it by transpiration. Some rainwater is lost because it evaporates immediately on falling on impermeable surfaces like the asphalt of roads and cities. Running water courses finally flow over saturated soils, shaping the complex systems of the watersheds or river basins.

Since each basin's natural system has developed gradually and has grown up according to the yearly distribution and fluctuations of rainfall, we have to appreciate that any large-scale project for redistributing water by means of pipes, as if it were gas or electricity, is a journey into the unknown. This is because it destroys the results of the work of shaping the climate, however transitory it might be.

Variable Volumes

All water supplies are of variable volume. Both the discharge of rivers and the level of lakes and aquifers depend on rainfall. As these resources are components of a large system, the river basin, a reasonable policy would be to manage water resources according to the characteristics of each basin. This would require, first of all, a proper understanding of the system so as to adapt use and consumption to the existing supply. Conserving river systems as much as possible in their natural state is the best guarantee for the preservation of the landscape and of a constant supply. Grondwater reservoirs aren't canals, but are more like lakes, so that pollution leads to the build-up of a debt which is paid in years to come.

Consumption

Water consumption has increased in recent years as a result of not only population growth but also an increase in living standards. In the rural areas the introduction of new farming methods, the spread of irrigation and the excessive use of fertilizers and pesticides causes very high consumption—it is estimated that more than 2/3 of water consumption is used in irrigating. Agricultural pollution also endangers both surface water and aquifers, which receive water full of chemical products. Many cases of eutrophication, the enrichment of water by nutrients that accelerate the growth of algae, derive from the run-off of fertilizers. The practice of intensive stock-raising on farms with large numbers of animals also brings about these problems of over consumption and pollution. Cleaning the stockyards requires large amounts of water which is then released into the environment with high concentrations of nitrogen.

As for industries, they have in the past taken little care over water consumption and dumping, and in many areas the need for proper attention comes as something new. The best thing would be to make industry take its water at a point down-river from where it returns it or, better still, generalise the use of closed circuit systems based on the constant recycling and reusing of the same water.

As regards human consumption, the general attitude to cleanliness is based on diluting pollutants. One example is the success of the use of the Water Closet which involves diluting a few decilitres of urine in 10 or more litres of drinking water: quite a record in wastefulness.

Another aspect to be considered is the different quality of the water that falls on well formed soils from the water that falls on roads, cities, airports, suburbs and built-up areas and whose composition is less stable and "worse" than that resulting from a more uniform interaction with mature soils. Remember that streets, roofs, communication routes, airports and built-up areas already cover a high proportion of the earth's land area and are still on the increase.

Purification techniques should be based especially on the natural processes that include biological activity. Otherwise—for example, if physico-chemical methods are used—there can be side-effects such as an excess of mud or sediments. The strategy to follow is to optimize operations in our use of water according to the discharge and to the distribution of contamination. A system in the form of a conduit or channel, such as a river, can respond relatively quickly. On the other hand, lakes and dams can only do so up to a point, because they show more inertia and irreversibility and take longer to clean.

Large lakes, not to mention the sea, might seem a good place to dump contaminating refuse, but they can't then be cleaned. This is the price we pass on the future generations: a comfortable attitude, but an unacceptable one.

26

Environmental Protection:

The Devil May Care

Back in the 1960s, most of us thought of the environment in terms of a medieval morality play. Thirty years later, those clear moral certainties are gone. Conservation has evolved into sustainable development (SD). And instead of denouncing the Devil of industry and all his works, the Goodies have become hopelessly ensnared in dialogue with him.

Most worrisome to all true believers, the debate between the SD movement and the private sector is proving remarkably fruitful. Indeed, this interface is the origin of many of the most interesting and provocative new ideas in sustainable development today.

The strategy of environmental protection in the 1970s relied overwhelmingly on government regulations and inspectors. Dubbed "Command-and-control" by business it involved government laying out detailed rules and using bureaucratic procedures to enforce them. Industry says that centralized hands-on regulation is inherently expensive and inefficient: the rules take so long to draw up that they impose standards that are two or more years out of date.

There are a number of reasons why command-and-control is no longer appropriate as a sole a primary strategy (except in some areas, such as nuclear power safety). Over the years, our concept of the proper role of the state has narrowed, with growing distaste for unnecessary bureaucratic control. And globalisation has created entirely new possibilities for market-based environmental management. A third reason is that the growth of civil society and its empowerment through the internet have substantially increased the risks to business of egregiously bad environmental behaviour. In most countries, environmental stupidity by industry is now likely to be exposed, and public pressure is able to insist on expensive remedies.

However, one factor stands out above all: the rule-book approach to the environment is just too expensive. Even the rich industrialized countries can't afford more and more regulations, inspectors and control boards. And for the developing world, using scarce skilled workers as environmental police seems even less practical. The tendency now in the major industrialized countries is for government to set performance goals, and to let industry decide how to reach them.

You just can't trust these guys, right? But consider how we make companies keep more or less honest books. We don't have vast numbers of accounts on the public payroll counting through; the receipts of everyone from Exxon to the corner store. The state lays down the basic book-keeping rules, and makes every business pay for an independent auditor to make sure that the rules are obeyed. Classic self-regulation, at little cost to the taxpayer.

Why not do the same for pollution control, product and workplace safety? A raft of pilot schemes is now under way to do just that that. For example, so far most self-regulating schemes lack transparency: they are not based on publicly available rules with published emissions levels. Nor are self-regulating companies usually accountable to anyone but themselves. These defects are recognized by some in industry, and attempt to correct them are being tested. So too is the concept of having such scheme formally registered with government, with legal or political sanctions for noncompliance.

Government likes self-regulation because it is cheap. And the SD lobby, somewhat unwillingly, is coming to accept this approach, especially for the developing world and "economies in transition". If Europe and NORTH America couldn't afford command-and-control, how can countries with far fewer lawyers, administrators, chemical engineers and lab workers? Business says that self-regulation leaves the private sector alone to do what it does best: finding the most cost-effective ways of reaching agreed goals.

Not everyone in the SD camp is happy with this increasingly close relationship. Some environmentalists question the motives of business. But in the end, these are irrelevant. What really matter is what business does.

Business motives for SD are complex, and public relations is certainly one of them. Another is staff recruitment and morale: people don't like working for a company that is perceived to be damaging the environment. There are straight bottom-line motives too: bad environmental performance can depress stock prices and cause boardroom firings. It is cheaper to design a new plant for environmental standards of tomorrow than to engage in expensive retrofits later. And reducing waste has often proved extemely profitable.

Profit. The environment and development movement used to see this a dirty word. But as these two groups melded into a single SD community, two key realisations started to emerge. The first was that sustainability does not ultimately depend on governments but on business, because business controls more than 90 per cent of the investment that shapes our future. The second was that business is based on profit so that achieving SD will require making sustainability profitable.

Making the profit motive work for sustainability is a carrot and stick affair - but without the stick the donkey would probably not go for the carrot.

In a competitive market, a boycott that cuts stales by a mere 10 per cent can make business hungry for the carrot. One promising carrot is eco-labeling, which enables consumers to make positive SD choices. The problem is to get producers, retailers, campaigners and consumers to agree on who gets this green stamp of approval. What exactly is an energy-efficient light bulb an organically grown pineapple or a sustainable logged armchair?

To someone reared on the view that you can't trust business at all sustainability initiatives seem to be cropping up in the oddest places. The world's insurance companies for example, are seriously worried about global warning, not just because it involves more storms, floods and severe weather, but because these events are unpredictable. Between 1991 and 1997, extreme weather cost the insurance industry US$200 billion, and companies fear that further rapid climate change could cause widespread bankruptcies. As a result, insurance has been lobbying for tighter controls on carbon dioxide than those agreed to in Kyoto.

Business and sustainable development remain uneasy bedfellows. But what cannot be denied is that the interface between them is spawning a wealth of intriguing ideas, insights and approaches.

This does not mean that civil society, governments and international institutions should be doing whatever business wants. On the contrary, as the private sector grows beyond the power of all but the largest states, the need for governmental and intergovernmental ground rules and for grassroots and international analysis, monitoring and criticism is more-urgent than ever. Market mechanisms and self-regulation are still in their infancy. But the pattern of government setting broad goals, and industry working out how to meet (or exceed) them, and being publicly accountable for doing so, will be centrally to SD in the 21st century.

27

The Environment, the Economy and Public Health:

An Integrated View

The environment is central to the health of people and their economies. Just as a foetus is totally dependent on the life-support system of the mother during her pregnancy, so the health and vitality of people and their economies are totally dependent on their environments. Unfortunately, many people do not see it that way. They either see the environment as dependent on the economy—such as the politician who says: "let's make the economy strong, then we'll fix the environment when we can afford it"—or they see little connection between health and the environment, whether they are "deep greens" campaigning on ecological issues or doctors treating individual patients and individual illnesses. Whether we are politicians, greens or doctors, is there not a more efficient way to fulfil our aims? For this, a broader perspective is essential.

All economies are sub-systems of the larger environmental system which provides the:

- sources of energy and materials;
- sinks for pollution and other wastes;
- services of water, nutrients and carbon recycling.
- space for living, working and aesthetics ("a walk in the woods and the song of a bird")

Neglect of this life-support system of the "4 S's" leads to weaker or defunct economies as vegetation, food, soils, water or air become contaminated or exhausted and gradually fail to support economic activity. This is dramatically illustrated in the Aral Sea region, or the collapsed Canadian salmon fishing communities.

Indirect Social Costs

Less catastrophic but still costly is where economic damage is caused by pesticides and nutrient contamination of groundwater, involving millions of Rupees in water treatment. This is a social cost to the economy that the agricultural sector does not include in the price of its food: an economic distortion that reduces the real wealth of society via false price signals that encourage the over-use of pesticides and fertilisers. Similarly, the "external" costs on society of road-respiratory-induced accidents, noise, respiratory and circulatory diseases and congestion amount to a lot of money to any government but these costs are not borne by transport users, which mean that transport is encouraged beyond the level that is economic for society as a whole. By internalising these externalities via taxes and other means, the market prices for transport would become fairer and more efficient. Currently only about 30 per cent of transport externalities are covered by transport taxes. But if the health of an economy is dependent on the health of its environment, what about the health of its people?

Without access to the basics of clean water, shelter, fresh air and food, people obviously suffer. Even in more developed economies where the link between everyday life and the environment is not so visible, the role of environmental factors in disease and well-being is significant. Most of the major diseases such as heart disease, cancer, respiratory diseases and allergies have an environmental as well as a genetic component within a multi-factorial chain of causation. And while each environmental factor may be small, if the links in the chain of causation are inter-dependent, as they often appear to be then removing even a small link can break the chain.

Environmental Factors

Take asthma in children, for example. These seem to be many causes, from a child's genetic inheritance to its nutritional status, which in turn help determine how it reacts to the many environmental factors, both indoor (such as mites, pets, damp, environmental tobaco smoke, nitrogen oxides) and outdoor (such as pollen and pollution from industry and traffic), that have been implicated in asthma causation. Therefore it is clear that diagnoses of asthma and many other diseases should systematically embrace environmental factors. This will be a significant challenge for doctors whose time is scarce and whose training is not usually appropriate.

This multi-causal chain will vary in its exact make-up from child to child, but for children overall, even if the evironmental factors such as damp housing to traffic fumes may be less important than, say, genetic make-up or nutritional status, the environmental factors may be the ones that can be most cost effectively removed, thus breaking the casual chain. And, as with many environmental issues, there are secondary benefits of action, such as less noise or fewer accidents from traffic reduction, or energy savings from dry houses, which further justify the environmental actions even where exact causations are not well understood.

The environmental causes of disease and ill health are a controversial and ill understood area of science and opinions vary about their significance. Some say that, for Western Europe, perhaps 2-3 per cent of public disease and ill-health is determined by known environmental factors but others maintain that it must be far more significant. They point to the sharp increase over the last two or three decades in asthma, allergies, and cancers (particularly of the productive organs such as breast and testicles) and related ill-health such as sperm count decline, which cannot be explained by genetic causes. They also observe that the large differences in health between the socio-economic classes cannot be explained without involving significant environmental causation.

It is thought that the ubiquitous presence of low doses of mixtures of chemicals in food, drink, air, consumer products and the general environment are playing some role in public ill health, even if the evidence for this is far from substantial.

Impact on Public Health

But what about environmental programmes and campaigns being little concerned with health? well, history so far shows that the environment only gets serious attention when it is seen to be damaging either the economy or public health. Yet because "everything connects" in "socio—enviro" systems, action to stop infectious diseases from water contamination, or to reduce skin cancer from ozone depletion, leads to a better environment for all species. And if upland forests are preserved because they are seen to be cheaper and more effective water regulators (which reduce the risk of lowland flooding) than dams, then upland biodiversity benefits anyway, even if it was last in the queue for political attention.

Although public health may be seen by some as only a small part of "the environment", much environmental progress depends upon the political weight of the health impacts. For example, the cost benefit exercise on the current multi-pollutant/effect programme on acidification, eutrophication and low-level ozone shows that it is the benefits to human health, not eco-system damage, that provide the main economic justification for further reductions in SO_2, No_x and NH_3. Ecologists need the language of public health in order to maximise political support for the environment. So, it is out of our specialist "boxes" of economics, health and ecology, and into a shared systems approach, with integrated programmes that build partnerships for progress.

28

Children's Health and the Environment

Children today live in an environment vastly different from that of a few generations ago. Economic development, increased urbanisation and the consequences of war in many countries have added to the traditional environmental hazards, those problems associated with environmental pollution. Thus, while some traditional children's diseases switch as diarrhea, malnutrition and infectious diseases persist in many countries, environmentally-related illnesses such as asthma, respiratory illness due to environmental tobacco smoke (ETS), as well as mortality and morbidity due to injuries, are increasing. In childhood cancer in some countries and the potential risks of endocrine-disrupting chemicals are among the emerging health threats that need careful vigilance. Children of lower socio-economic status are likely to suffer disproportionately from all these health threats as a consequence of living in highly polluted environments, poor quality housing, lower levels of education, and of restricted access to environmental and health care services.

Children's Vulnerability

The concern for children's vulnerability to environmental health threats is based on several factors. Children receive greater exposures than adults do because they drink more water, eat more food and have higher breathing rates per unit of body weight. Because they are undergoing rapid growth and development, toxicant effects at specific times may have irreversible consequences. For example, if vital connections between nerve cells fail to form during brain development, there is high risk that the resulting neurobehavioral dysfunction will be permanent and irreversible. Also, because most children have more future years of life than adults, they have more time to develop any chronic disease that may be triggered by early environmental exposures.

Public Health Threats

Asthma, injuries, and the effects of environmental tobacco smoke (ETS) are among the most significant public health threats to children. Childhood asthma is increasingly prevalent in all most all countries. What causes asthma is not known, but several environmental factors, such as indoor air quality (particularly exposure to the house-dust mite) and ETS, have been linked with the increase in asthma. In addition, outdoors air pollutants such as particulates; sulphur dioxide and ozone exacerbate asthma symptoms. ETS, especially smoking by the mother, is a known risk factor for asthma. ETS is also known to cause acute and chronic middle ear disease and is associated with sudden infant death syndrome (SIDS).

Potential for Prevention

The variation in asthma and injury rates and the evidence of the role of certain environmental factors underline the potential for prevention. Public policies should seek to avoid preventable childhood diseases by preventing exposures to environmental agents and considering children's characteristics and susceptibilities in the development of environmental health legislation. Promoting citizen awareness and participation in policy-making through education and access to environmental information are important elements in achieving a safe environment for children. In this context, children are not only consumers with rights, but also citizens who can play an active role towards their own protection.

International Awareness

Several international agreements have acknowledged children's vulnerabilities and have committed their signatories to protect children's health form the effects of a deteriorating environment. This year, many countries will address several of the environmental health threats to children through international and national action. It is expected that a large international collaborative initiative will result under the guidance of WHO and other international organisations.

29

Population and the Environment:

The Global Challenge

As the century begins, natural resources are under increasing pressure, threatening public health and development. Water shortages, soil exhaustion, loss of forests, air and water pollution, and degradation of coastlines afflict many areas. As the world's population grows, improving living standards without destroying the environment is a global challenge.

Most developed economies currently consume resources much faster than they can regenerate. Most developing countries with rapid population growth face the urgent need to improve living standards. As we humans exploit nature to meet present needs, are we destroying resources needed for the future?

Environment Getting Worse

In the past decade in every environmental sector, conditions have either failed to improve, or they are worsening:

Public Health. Unclean water, along with poor sanitation, kills over 12 million people each year, most in developing countries. Air pollution kills nearly 3 million more. Heavy metals and other contaminants also cause widespread health problems.

Food Supply. Will there be enough food to go around? In 64 of 105 developing countries studies by UN Food and Agricultural organisation the population has been growing faster than food supplies. Population pressures have degraded some 2 billion hectares of arable land—an area the size of Canada and the US.

Fresh Water. The supply of fresh water is finite, but demand is soaring as population grows and use per capita rises. By 2025, when world population is projected to be 8 billion, 48 countries, containing 3 billion people will face shortages.

Coastlines and Oceans. Half of all coastal ecosystems are pressured by high population densities and urban development. A tide of pollution is rising in the world's seas. Ocean fisheries are being overexploited, and fish catches are down.

Forests. Nearly half of the world's original forest cover has been lost, and each year another 16 million hectares are cut, bulldozed, or burned. Forests provide over US$400 billion to the world economy annually and are vital to maintaining healthy ecosystems. Yet, current demand for forest products may exceed the limit of sustainable consumption by 25 per cent.

Biodiversity. The earth's biological diversity is crucial to the continued vitality of agriculture and medicine and perhaps even to life on earth itself. Yet human activities are pushing many thousands of plant and animal species into extinction. Two of every three species is estimated to be in decline.

Global Climate Change. The earth's surface is warming due to greenhouse gas emissions, largely from burning fossil fuels. If the global temperature rises as projected, sea levels would rise by several meters, causing widespread flooding. Global warming also could cause droughts and disrupt agriculture.

Toward a Livable Future

How people preserve or abuse the environment could largely determine whether living standards improve or deteriorate. Growing human numbers, urban expansion, and resource exploitation do not bode well for the future. Without practicing sustainable development, humanity faces a deteriorating environment and may even invite ecological disaster.

Taking Action. Many steps toward sustainability can be taken today. These include using energy more efficiently; managing cities better; phasing out subsidies that encourage waste; managing water resources and protecting fresh water sources; harvesting forest products rather than destroying forests; preserving arable land and increasing food production through a second Green Revolution; managing coastal zones and ocean fisheries; protecting biodiversity hotspots; and adopting an international convention on climate change.

Stabilizing Population. While population growth has slowed, the absolute number of people continues to increase 0 by about 1 billion every 13 years, slowing population growth would help improve living standards and would buy time to protect natural resources. In the long run, to sustain higher living standards world population size must stabilize.

30

Sustainable Tourism and the Environment

Tourism is high on the international agenda. The 7th session of the Commission on Sustainable Development focused on tourism and subsequently work programmes on sustainable tourism are being developed. Also the Convention on Biological Diversity is embarking on tourism programmes and bilateral and multilateral financial institutions placed tourism high on their priority lists. The UN declared 2002 as the International Year of Ecotourism and the World Tourism Organisation adopted a Global Code of Ethics for Tourism at its General Assembly, held in Santiago de Chile.

The World Tourism Organisation forecasts that there will be 702 million international arrivals in the year 2002, that arrivals will top 1 billion in the year 2010 and that by 2020 international arrivals will reach 1.6 billion—nearly three times the number of international trips made in 1996, which was 592 million.

Travellers of the 21st century will go farther and farther. The Tourism 2020 Vision forecast predicts that by 2020 one out of every three trips will be a long haul journey to another region of the world. It is expected that China will become a major force in international tourism and the WTO predicts that about 100 million Chinese will take international trips by 2020, thus putting them in fourth place in numbers of travellers after Germany, Japan and the United States. By the same time, China will attract 137 million visitors—63.5

million overseas visitors travelled to China in 1998 and thus outrank France as the world's top destination. It is estimated that during 1999 France will receive a record number of tourists of more than 70 million; in 2007 France hopes to attract 90 million visitors. The key resource for the most popular tourist destinations is the most popular tourist destinations is the natural environment: coastal resorts, tropical rainforests, wildlife in national parks and alpine skiresorts, all rely on a mixture of natural beauty, good weather and safe condition to attract holiday destination is landscape and natural environment, followed by climate, the cost of the journey and the historical features of the place to visit, hence, conserving the ecological integrity and environment is imperative if tourism is to be sustained.

The pressure from millions of tourists on water and marine resources, on land and landscape, wildlife and habitat is enormous and often has devastating impact on the environment and the local population who are increasingly deprived of access to clean water and other natural resources.

In some regions, particularly in small island countries, tourism is one of the major reasons for wasting and polluting water: on average one tourist consumes at least 6 times more water than a local resident.

Major waters waster and polluter are golf courses. In many countries, golf has brought heavy ecological and social costs: deforestation, the destruction of bio-diversity and erosion; dispossession of peoples' homes and farms; over-consumption and pollution of water and very high use of pesticides and fertilisers which threaten local residents, workers, wildlife and the golfers themselves. A survey by the Japanese National Doctors Health Insurance Association has revealed that many golfers, caddies and residents living near a golf course suffer from skin inflammation, disorders of the ear, nose and throat and other respiratory illnesses to the inhalation of pesticides because up to 90 per cent of the chemicals sprayed on golf courses end up in the air. In some areas in Thailand, diseases emerged which, prior to the construction of golf courses, had not been known.

In some regions, golf courses have depleted water supply, agricultural production has come to a halt, peasants have become impoverished and forced to migrate to urban areas in search of employment. Golf courses take large amounts of land. It is estimated that each year world wide up to 5,000 hectares of forest are cut to clear land for golf courses.

Very often, the construction of golf courses forms an integral part of a comprehensive tourism project. Adjacent to the golf course condominiums and/or hotels are built, very often also a marina, an airport and a casino. Studies have shown that such a complex not only has touristic objective but is often connected to drug trafficking and money-laundering. Even the US State Department has emphasized the link between tourism, money-laundering and offshore banking.

Cruise ships are a major cause for pollution in the Caribbean, destroying maritime life and reefs by releasing waste into the ocean. Recently the Royal Caribbean, the world's second largest cruise line was fined a record sum of US$ 18 million of dumping waste oil and hazardous chemicals into the sea. The company admitted to routinely dumping wasted oil from its fleet and that it deliberately dumped in U.S. harbors and coastal areas many other types of pollutants, including hazardous chemicals from photo processing equipment, dry cleaning shops and printing presses. Some hazardous materials, including toxic solvents from dry cleaning operations, were illegally placed in the garbage aboard the ships. The material was then either incinerated on the ship or dumped in U.S. or foreign ports mixed with ordinary garbage.

It was announced that the Royal Caribbean Cruise reported a profit of US$ 338 million in 1997, a 93 per cent increase over the previous year, Carnival Corporation's Holland, the biggest cruise company with a turnover of US$ 3 billion in 1997 made a net profit of US $836 million, 25 per cent more than in 1996. Both cruise companies have recently been fined millions of dollars for dumping untreated bilge water, oil and other waste into Alaskan waters.

However, the impact of oil and hazardous waste on water, maritime life and coral reefs is devastating and all fines paid for the damage caused by the cruise ships will not revive dead corals.

A recent Green peace study on coral reefs—one of the marine world's great natural treasure—predicts that the coral bleaching which dramatically whitened many of the world's reefs last year will escalate rapidly under accepted global climate models and that the damage would wreak havoc in fisheries and tourism, disrupting the economies of many nations.

A WWF study recently published on "Climate Change and its Impacts on Tourism", warned that droughts, rising seas, flash floods, forest fires and diseases could turn profitable destinations into holiday horror stories. The report urges the tourist industry to persuade western industrialised governments to take more concerted action to reduce their nations' carbon dioxide emissions the main cause of global warming.

The Need for Action and Education

If government, the international community and the tourism industry want to save the world's major tourist destinations, immediate action is required. Governments and the tourism industry must abide to the principle that environmental protection is an integral part of tourism development. In order to protect the environment and mitigate the damages caused by tourism, some countries have decided to take action: The Spanish Island Minorca and the Seychelles will introduce Eco-tax on tourism. This tax will be around US $ 12 per person in Minorca and its revenues are earmarked for the maintenance of national parks and the restoration of damaged coastline. Visitors to the Seychelles will have to buy a so-called "gold-card" at a price of 100 $ which entitles unlimited access to the country; income from this card will be used for sewage management and protection of fresh water supply.

Only if tourism investor and developers:

(a) consider the natural capacity for the regeneration and future productivity of natural resources.

(b) recognise the contribution that people and communities, customs and life styles make to the tourism experience and therefore accept that these people must have an equitable share in the economic benefits of tourism; and

(c) listen to local people in the tourist destinations, tourism may become sustainable.

Education and awareness raising campaigns at all levels are therefore imperative.

31

Urbanisation and the Environment

Is abandoning the cities the answer to the growing ecological problems of urbanisation? The trend at any rate is in the opposite direction. At the beginning of this century, only every 10th person worldwide was a city dweller. At its end, more than half the global population will be urbanites. And most of the urban population growth will take place in the developing countries, led by Asia.

Compared to other parts of the world, however, the urbanisation process in Asia is currently not even particularly far out in front. Worldwide, city dwellers account for 43 per cent of the total population. Industrial nations have an average urbanisation rate of 72 per cent. Less industrialized countries have 34 per cent. In the Asia-Pacific region the rate is 30 per cent, in Latin America 72 per cent, and in Africa 33 per cent. The urbanisation growth rate in a number of Asian countries has in fact slowed compared with earlier years. Nevertheless, not only industrialisation, but also the increasing degree of urbanisation has emerged as a growing burden on the environment in many Asian countries.

Changed Urbanisation Pattern in India

Environment burdens are just as much a problem in the old industrial nations as they are in India. But each group has a specific pattern of development. The urbanisation process in India has proven to be more pollution-intensive than that in the old industrial nations of Europe and North America. There are several reasons for that:

industrialisation in India is restricted to a few locations which are often concentrated in and around capital cities. Although environmental damage continues to be minor at a national level, these locations have higher pollution levels than those ever reached in Industrial nations;

- furthermore, besides the strong regionalisation of industries, the industrialisation pattern of India shows a great diversity of environmental hazards. The trend to establish "last industries first", which is promoted by progressive industrialisation, leads to a country producing certain dangerous materials before they have been covered by state regulations;
- the time factor has to be seen as an important element in the emergence of these already highly regionalized environmental burdens. In India industrialisation and its concomitant urbanisation is taking place within a ban population grew tremendously.

Growing Environmental Damage

Water pollution in India is caused mainly by domestic sewage. For example, households are responsible for 75 per cent of the pollution of the rivers. The domestic sewage problem got more and more out of control with growing urban population. Pipe-based waste water systems are rare in this country. In India dealing with waste has an extremely low priority. The type of waste disposal depends mostly on what the cities can afford. The present level of air pollution is also very high.

Innovative Approaches to Solutions

Environmental protection and economic development are seen as contradictions. Economic development can only be achieved at the cost of higher levels of environmental pollution. And in reverse, if pollution is to be controlled and reduced this can only be done to the disadvantage of further development. In the meantime, however, numerous instances of successful urban environmental management are developing. They could help to change and subsequently break through the existing pattern of thinking. The following approaches can be viewed as important.

Combining regulations with incentives: The introduction of lead-free petrol and the mandatory equipping of new cars with catalytic converters is still by no means common in India. As numerous cars without catalytic converters are still able to use lead-free. Converters were then at first made compulsory for higher-powered cars, and later also for compact models.

Combining regulations with simple controls: Apart from general limitation of the number of cars in the city, its most important single measure to prevent traffic jams and the additional petrol consumption and pollutant emissions caused by them.

High economic growth in India has in fact led to a general reduction of poverty. But the distribution of income, particularly between urban and rural areas, has remained relatively constant. Urban environmental and traffic problems have increased heavily during the same period. These developments can be attributed to a certain pattern of official action (or "non-action"):

- governments have made efforts in supplying roads, but neglected the demand for mobility.
- governments are preoccupied with supplying water, and have neglected follow up problems, above all the questions of waste water disposal and treatment. In Indian cities, for example, this leads to the absurd situation that due to the mushroom like growth of the cities and the increased water pollution linked with it, water must be brought in over ever greater distances and at ever greater expense;
- governments take a one-sided look at noxious substances. Concentrations of harmful substances in water and in the air are in fact checked, and some measures are taken against individual pollutants of

single sectors (e.g. lead emissions by the transport sector).

But an integrated policy which operates integrated environmental management with the aim of comprehensively relieving the burdens on the environment has not yet been developed anywhere. To consider such a concept, it is necessary to cut loose from the customary way of approaching problems. It makes sense not to separate the problem areas from each other according to sectors and pollutants, but rather on the basis of their ecological impact.

Orienting on demand hits the core of the concept of ecological modernisation, which is about reducing the intensity of resource use (note, at this stage this does not yet mean the absolute reduction of inputs). At the same time, sights are set on a lower use of land with the same size of population, or also lower energy consumption with the same degree of added value or the same per capita income.

Finally, the importance of governments for creating framework conditions must be emphasised once again. Because the actors come from different spheres, such conditions are essential.

From the time of the Greek polis, it was the ambition of the Greek city councillors to pass on a city that was more beautiful than the one they had taken over. There is a long way to go before such an attribute asserts itself in India (and elsewhere).

32

Economics and Sustainable Development

Economists and ecologists were once seen as enemies: environmental protection, it was thought, could only be achieved at the expense of economic growth. The misconception persists at the extremes among both the most fundamentalist Greens and the most ideological free marketers. But increasingly it is now being recognised that development and care for the environment go hand in hand. This interdependence is coalescing in the new and necessary discipline of environmental economics.

Conventional economics patterns have often assumed that growth and technical progress will nullify all resource and environmental limits. Environmental economics recognises that the world's natural capital underpins all development, and that it is rapidly becoming scarcer as human demands exceed the globe's long-term carrying capacity. Government of India has introduced environmental measures over the last two decades, but need to move further towards integrating them into economic policies. There can be no real sustainable development unless environment and development policies are integrated at the very beginning of the decision-making process.

Quantifying the Environmental Cost

One of the first steps is to work out the true costs of polluting and depleting the World's natural resources, such as its soil, air and water, the climate and the ozone layer. There have often been regarded as free goods, and it was believed that the world has an infinite capacity to absorb the effects of human activities. Environmental economists, recognising that the social and economic costs of degradation are very great, are trying to quantify them. They say that this will make possible better use of such tools as cost-benefit analysis, environmental impact assessment and risk assessment—and the production of national income accounts which reflect the depletion and degradation of natural resources. As these costs are identified and quantified, economic policy can increasingly be developed with sustainable development as the primary objective. Achieving sustainable development requires industrialized and developing countries to make dramatic changes in national and international policies based on a global partnership. The greenhouse effect, the destruction of the ozone layer, the extinction of species and contamination of the oceans, and other environmental problems, affect us all, no matter which corner of the globe we inhabit.

The first and essential step in overcoming a difficulty is to recognize it and understand it. Concern over the difficulties related to sustainability has led scientists and national and international institutions to study the concept and suggest ways of meeting its many requirements. Indicators have been established to measure pollution levels, soil erosion, salinisation, deforestation an a host of environmental problems. Evaluating the impact of such natural resource-use on ecosystems is a major step towards finding the true necessary solutions.

For example, it has become clear, on a macroeconomic level, that national accounting systems fail to reflect these effects adequately, Deterioration of the world's rivers, land degradation, air pollution and contamination of the seas are not taken into consideration. Inadequate accounting distorts reality and gives a false idea of the consequences of growth and production.

On a microeconomic level, much is being done to redefine production costs. Incorporating the cost of waste management and internalizing negative external impacts within production prices are beneficial aspects of the economics of sustainability.

Steps are being taken to evaluate public and commonly held assets and to put a price on them, even though they may not be subject to market forces. These are only in the earliest stage but they will allow for more accurate evaluation of the world's natural capital. Fiscal, market, quota and other instruments are being developed to enforce change in the way in which certain resources are used. Examples include markets for transferable emission quotas or compensatory taxation mechanisms designed to ensure that economic forces act to reduce greenhouse gas emissions. Efforts at impact analysis and in a general sense, cost-benefit analysis permit rough estimations of the impact that projects might have no ecosystems.

Long-term Repercussions

These instruments carry significant limitations but they are important nevertheless because they attempt to quantify impacts on the natural world and to achieve a more rational use of natural resources. The development of such instruments and evaluation techniques will have significant repercussions in the formulation of sustainable long-term policies. But we must bear in mind that sustainability is not just an economic issue: it is also a political and cultural one.

The concept of sustainability demands as alternative view point in which humankind and the natural world are perceived as a unit—as different yet mutually sustaining aspects of a whole. This perception is not incompatible with progress. It does not renounce development. It simply seeks to affirm life and refuses to discriminate between the means and the end.

It understands that happiness cannot be achieved by destructive means. The questions of how to produce and how to consume therefore become extremely important. Neither should be at the expense of the future or of the natural world. Efficiency is not limited to the links between investment, products and prices: it must address the rational use of resources, including environmental and cultural consequences, both in the long and the shot-term.

Very considerable adjustments must be made in the interests of sustainable development. They demand a reassessment of all our activities which cannot, logically, be done overnight. It is a long continuous process, characterised by steadfastness and compromise.

33

Sustainable Cities

Today almost one half of the world's population lives in cities. The world's cities are growing by one million people each week. Cities today play a significant role in development. They continue to attract migrants from rural areas because they enable people to advance socially and economically. Cities offer significant economies of scale in the provision of jobs, housing and services, and are important centres of productivity and social development.

However, the stress of this rapid urban population growth is often overwhelming. The long list of afflictions includes urban poverty rates of up to 60 per cent. Despite growing investments, more than one third of the urban population live in substandard housing. Forty per cent of urban dwellers do not have access to safe drinking water or adequate sanitation. Primarily due to a rapid growth and a deteriorating urban environment, at least 600 million people in human settlements (cities, towns and villages) already live in health and life threatening situations, and almost 50 per cent of these are children.

The high rate of urban population growth in most regions has led to common problems: congestion, lack of funds to provide basic services, a shortage of adequate housing and declining infrastructure, to name a few.

While these problems are occurring in urban areas, cities still have an important role to play in protecting the global environment in the face of rapid urban population growth.

Agricultural and livestock production in rural areas are pushing farther and farther into ecologically fragile regions and cannot support growing population. The finite land and water resources make it imperative that human settlements be carefully planned. Indeed, sustainable urbanisation will ease the pressures caused by encroachment on fragile natural habitats.

India's cities offer a bewildering sight to any visitor: the congestion caused by rapid population growth and a continuing rural-urban drift often leads to conditions which defy all rules of orders, hygiene and environmental safety. Inadequate leadership, corruption and mismanagement have a harmful effect on the physical, environmental, social and ethical structures of cities in India.

Millions of people live in inadequate conditions—without piped water, electricity, security of land tenure, access to roads or health facilities. The means available for production and financing of housing and urban infrastructure are too limited to meet basic needs.

Reducing Poverty and Creating Jobs

Urban poverty is rising at an alarming pace, especially among women. The informal economic sector—which makes a substantial contribution to the delivery of services, production of goods, building of infrastructure and housing construction—often provides the only opportunity for the urban poor to make a living.

Local informal housing construction, for example, generates up to 20 per cent more jobs than high-cost construction. Street hawking, waste recycling and food production are primary sources of income among the urban poor and are illustrative of the creativity of survival strategies.

However, the informal sector itself is often highly exploitative and fails to raise people's economic development beyond mere subsistence. Larger economic strategies and more participatory urban planning approaches that take stock of local skills, technologies and materials are required to generate new and better-paying job opportunities in cities and towns.

Incorporating Environmental Concerns

In 1992 the Rio Conference on Environment and Development designed the Agenda 21 Programme of Action to help save a planet endangered by environmental neglect and plagued by poverty and underdevelopment. Most of the goals agreed to in Rio can become reality only through local action in cities where environmental threats are increasing. Again, it is the urban poor who are particularly endangered by environmental degradation and pollution. The world's Agenda 21 will fail if the city's environmental agenda (population, inadequate sanitation, water supply and waste management) is not addressed. This is being recognised by local authorities all over the world.

Sustainable development in the twenty first century will to a large degree, depend upon how cities, towns and villages everywhere interact with the environment and utilize natural resources.

Increasing Awareness of Gender issues

Women and men use and experience cities differently, according to their roles, responsibilities and access to resources. For example, when basic services are lacking in a settlement, more often than not it is women who take on responsibilities such as water collection and refuse disposal. Women often have unequal access to resources such as property, credit, training and technology. All of these factors must be addressed urgently, as they make it harder for women to improve their living standards and those of their children.

Disaster Mitigation Relief and Reconstruction

As cities become large and more densely populated, they become increasingly vulnerable to natural and man-made disasters such as earthquake, floods, industrial hazards, epidemics, civil strife and wars. Poor people are forced to live in the most exposed, dangerous and cramped conditions; in flood-prone areas, on steep hillsides or near polluted streams and waste dumps. As a result, they are most likely to lose their homes or their lives when disasters occur. Better planning, access to affordable urban land, and improved construction methods can reduce the extent of catastrophes.

These successful and sustainable approaches to poverty eradication; managing the urban environment; providing access to land, shelter and finance; empowering women and men; and many other issues will have to be documented and disseminated widely.

34
Pollution for Export

After tax havens ... pollution havens? Are multinationals seeking to relocate in countries with low environmental standards? It all depends on how you look at it. In the search for new sources of capital, labour and raw materials are multinational corporations looking to relocate in "pollution havens" where environmental regulations are lax if not non-existent?

The question is increasingly being asked at a time when the level of foreign direct investment (FDI) is rising sharply. This is mainly due to the fact that both "source" and "host" countries recognize that each have something to gain from the FDI process. However, some observers are afraid that economic gains are being generated at the expense of environmental quality and other important elements of social welfare. They worry that "host" countries will compete for the benefits of new FDI by lowering their environmental standards or by reducing efforts to enforce existing standards, and that firms will relocate to these "pollution havens", to gain a cost advantage over their competitors. In this scenario, developing countries are regarded as the most likely sites of pollution havens because they may be the countries most willing to trade off their environmental quality for economic gains, and industrialised countries are cast in the role of predators willing to degrade the environment of developing countries in order to generate economic gains for themselves. However, most research suggests that, overall, companies do not invest overseas to obtain access to lower environmental costs.

It is difficult to determine whether FDI flows are affected by the level of environmental regulations existing in foreign countries. Foreign capital clearly flows to a wide range of countries, industries and companies some of which are careful environmental stewards, some of which are not. A firm may in any case invest in a country to take advantage of a high quality labour force and other factors unrelated to environmental costs.

Respect for the Environment: A Good Selling Point

Environmental costs are often a relatively small component of total production costs, which may sometimes even be lower when environmental standard are higher (for example, where lower environmental standards lead to higher costs of treating industrial water supplies).

Multinationals often seem more interested in consistent enforcement of environmental rules than in lower standards per se. Moreover, companies are often willing to make new investments that actually improve the environment, so long as their main competitors are also required to do so. Part of the reason for this is that multinational frequently apply a single environmental standard to their world-wide operations, regardless of any (lower) standards which may exist in a particular country. There could be three main reasons for this.

First, the firm may have calculated that it cannot afford to see the reputation of its products in the (global) market-place tarnished by charges of "environmental exploitation" in one particular location-charges which can sometimes result in boycotts or other forms of consumer pressure. For example, investors in Puerto Rican banana production firms have insisted on "due environmental care" by those firms, because they perceive that overseas markets for their products will demand higher levels of environmental quality.

Second, the firm may have calculated that it is less expensive to apply a single environmental standard to its (globally integrated) production processes, rather than to develop 'tailor-made" production lines, based on varying levels of environmental standards.

Finally, the ability of firms to make "dirty" investments may be limited by requirements in their home country. For example, the US Ex-Im Bank requires any US company taking advantage of its export financing assistance to meet certain minimum environmental criteria.

On the other hand, there is some evidence to suggest that "pollution havens" do exist within certain types of firms, operating in specific industries, and in particular countries. Investments made in the resource extraction and processing sectors, such as chemicals, metallurgy, logging, and pulp and paper, fall into this category. In these industries, pollution control costs can make up a significant proportion of the firm's total costs. The result can be that small cost differences can translate into large changes in market share and profitability. These firms are more susceptible to the level of environmental costs, and therefore more likely to invest in "pollution havens". However, this does not necessarily mean that countries actually lower their environmental standards to attract new investments.

There is clearly competition, both within and between countries, to obtain access to new FDI. It is particularly keen in the rapidly-industrializing countries, and in countries which are dependent on the resource extraction and processing industries in which the potential for hard currency export earnings may be very high. In these situations, incoming investors can often successfully argue for relief from "high" environmental costs.

But surprising though it may seem, investors in resource-based industries do not always exert pressures for lower environmental standards—sometimes they may even want standards in the host country to be raised.

Competitive pressures can also translate into a desire to reduce waste and improve productivity, which can lead to improved environmental performance. An ethic of eco-efficiency, which seeks to "design out" pollution problems rather than deal with unwanted waste, is increasingly accepted.

FDI is also often associated with modern technologies which represent environmental improvements over what is currently available in the host country. Once the investment has been made, local firms may try to imitate multinationals' environmental practices. But there is also evidence that certain kinds of enterprises (e.g. the town and village enterprises of rural China) seen prone to use outdated technical equipment from other countries that does not represent the "best environmental technology", because they are undercapitalized and because this equipment is cheap.

There is also some evidence that "pollution havens" may be associated with something other than the level of environmental standards. For example, pollution intensities did appear to increase more rapidly in Latin America as a whole between 1970 and 1990, after environmental regulations in OECD countries became stricter. But it was not the countries with the lowest environmental standards which attracted the most pollution intensive investment, it was those countries which were less open to FDI in the first place. "Pollution havens" were found, but they seemed to be more closely associated with protectionism economies than with lower environmental standards.

Overall, countries which operate straight forward, transparent, and efficient environmental programmes seem to experience no particular loss of FDI flows, and may in fact attract some industries which are looking for reliable overseas bases of operation. In short, governments are recognising that lowering environmental standards to attract new FDI is often unnecessary.

35
Living with Diversity

Fishers' nets and loggers' saws may directly impoverish local ecosystems, but most biological losses have root causes far away, in long-settled urban areas and farms where diversity is seldom a concern, but where steadily rising demand for food, water, wood and other resource and the dispersal of resulting wastes reach far beyond the settled areas themselves. In general, these peopled landscapes have lost much of their own biological wealth, but what remains is still important to their continued functioning and livability. Reconciling farms and cities with diversity will require stopping the damage they bring to remaining natural habitats, but also beginning to halt and reverse the homogenisation of these unnatural habitats.

Uniformity is not inherently undesirable. In fact, to some degree, homogeneity is the basis of all agriculture: a given type of plant is favorued and others are suppressed or eliminated. But trends in recent decades (most notably the Green Revolution and the parallel intensification of farming systems in industrial nations) have pushed uniformity to dangerous levels.

The unsustainability of modern agriculture is in part a measure of its inability to tolerate diversity. Both genetic and ecological uniformity—the sameness of fields sown horizon to horizon without interruption—demand costly and often futile reliance on chemicals to protect crops from pests or diseases that are rapidly spreading and evolving. The drive to leave no hectare unplowed worsens soil erosion, pushing tractors onto highly erodible hillsides and removing windbreaks, hedgerows and other remnant habitats.

Some of agriculture's biological impacts are obvious—the expansion of farms onto forests and wetlands, for example. While the increasing reliance on chemical inputs and machinery has reduced these impacts in some cases by decreasing the area needed to produce a given amount of food, it has worsened others.

A fundamental transition away from today's wasteful and polluting farming systems is needed to put the world's food supplies on a secure footing. Many of the reforms that will reduce farming's dependence on fossil fuel inputs and its misuse of soils and waters can also restore diversity to agricultural landscapes. Pesticides, for example, kill not only pests but other animals, such as pollinators and predators, that are beneficial to agriculture. Alternative pest control measures that lower pesticide use can also, ironically, reduce pest damage to crops by reviving the diversity of soil and insect communities, which play crucial roles in maintaining soil productivity and checking the spread of pest outbreaks.

Traditional agroecosystems are important not only because they provide sustenance to rural people and harbour valuable genetic resources, but also because they contain the seeds of a sustainable, diversity-based mode of agriculture. At varying levels, diversity is the basis of production for many peasants. Farmers often mix strains of a given crop in their fields as a hedge against the vagaries of weather. They also tend to recognize the dependence of their farms on adjacent ecological systems and to tolerate wild plants (often crop relatives whose continued interbreeding with domestic descendants contributes to genetic variety) on the outskirts of their fields.

Population growth and the expansion of large commercial farms have rendered many once-sound practices no loner viable, and traditional agriculture badly needs infusions of money and research to increase its modest yields without abandoning its stability.

Urban areas, with good reason, are considered the antithesis of natural diversity. Only the most resilient creatures (many of them regarded as weeds and pests) thrive in them, and cities' ceaseless expansion, consumption of resources, and emissions of waste threaten both farmland and wilderness almost everywhere. As with agricultural lands, the first priority for urban areas is to half their expansion onto other ecosystems and reduce the damage they export, such as the sewage poured onto coral reefs by burgeoning coastal cities throughout the tropics, or the wasteful consumption of tropical hardwoods in Japanese building construction.

But even concrete jungles can support some diversity. Landscaping of private yards and public spaces with native vegetation can not only reduce the expense and environmental impact of watering, spraying and hauling the remains of sterile grass monocultures, but also help revive bird and other wildlife populations. Most urban areas also have water-ways running through them, or corridors of unused land such as steep ravines; if their use as waste receptacles is reduced, these can be maintained or restored as wildlife habitat.

In developing nations, especially, a surprising amount of agricultural production takes place within city limits, in home gardens. These hidden farmlands contain a great deal of genetic diversity, and their expansion could help reduce the scale and environmental impacts of commercial agriculture.

One reason that the destruction of biological diversity has gone so far without major public commitments to stopping it is that urban dwellers have little experience of the natural and even less understanding of its importance. Restoring nature where people live-reestablishing a personal link with the living world may be necessary to save it elsewhere. For all the rational arguments favouring long-term protection of biological assets, people who have lost all direct sense of their dependence on natural systems may simply not care.

Only a growing respect for diversity for its own sake—beginning, perhaps, with a reconnection between people and nature within the urban environment—will trigger altruistic responses among those wealthy enough to have the option of considering the needs of future generations and natural communities. Although many conservation measures make economic sense, arguments of economics or self-interest will likely fail to be convincing when the contest is between a few uncharismatic species of unknown value and a major industrial project. "Human beings make sacrifices for what they love." Those who maintain strong bonds with the biological world on which they depend may be more inclined to make the hard decisions needed to protect it.

36

Biodiversity

As human population has surged this century, the populations of numerous other species have tumbled, many to the point of extinction. Indeed, we live amid the greatest extinction of plant and animal life since the dinosaurs disappeared some 65 million years ago, with species losses at 100 to 1,000 times the natural rate. But humans are not just witnesses to a rare historic event, we are actually its cause. The leading sources of today's species loss, habitat alteration, invasions by exotic species, pollution, and overhunting are all a function of human activities.

Human activities have pushed the percentage of mammals, amphibians, land fish that are in "immediate danger" of extinction into double digits. The principal cause of species extinction is habitat loss—the result of encroachment by humans for settlements, for agriculture, or to claim resources such as timber. A particularly productive but vulnerable habitat is found in coastal areas, home to 60 per cent of the world's population. Coastal wetlands nurture two thirds of all commercially caught fish, for example. And coral reefs have the second highest concentration of biodiversity in the world, after tropical reinforests. But human encroachment and pollution are degrading these areas: roughly half of the world's salt marshes and mangrove swamps have been eliminated or radically altered, and two thirds of the world's coral reefs have been degraded, 10 per cent of them "beyond recognition". As coastal migration continues—coastal dwellers could account for 75 per cent of world population within 30 years—the pressures on these productive habitats will likely increase".

Habitat loss tends to accelerate with an increase in a country's population density. This is bad news for the world's biodiversity hotspots-species-rich ecosystems at greatest risk of destruction. Twenty-four of these hotspots, containing half of the planet's species, have been identified globally. Some of the most important hotspot countries will reach population densities that have been linked with very high rates of habitat loss. Five of the six most biologically rich countries could see more than two thirds of their original habitat destroyed by 2050 if this historical relationship holds.

Related to loss of habitat is the growing incidence of plant, animal, insect, and microbial invasions of ecosystems worldwide as human interchange increases. These "exotic species" sometimes dominate local ecosystems, eliminating native species and reducing overall diversity. Exotics are implicated in 68 per cent of all fish exticntions in the United States this century, for example. Growth in human travel and commerce explains many accidental invasions by exotics, but foreign species are also deliberately introduced into farms, plantation forests, and aquaculture systems. Although only 1 per cent of exotics cause widespread damage, exotic species are the second leading cause, after habitat destruction, of species loss worldwide.

Other, often diffuse effects of expanded human activities also disrupt ecosystems. Nitrogen, for example, is now made available to plants at more than twice the preindustrial rate as a result of fertilizer production, cultivation of nitrogen-fixing crops, and the burning of fossil fuels. This overfertilisation of the Earth favours some species at the expense of others, leading to a reduction in diversity and resiliency of land and aquatic ecosystems.

Likewise, greenhouse gas emissions could disrupt ecosystems on a vast scale. As with nitrogen, increased levels of atmospheric carbon may favour some species over others: annuals over perennials, for example, or deciduous trees over evergreens. To the extent that greenhouse gases induce changes in global climate, many species may be at risk as habitats shift or shrink, and as some life forms, such as insects or animals, adapt and migrate more quickly than others, such as plants. And as sea levels rise with a change in climate, ecosystems such as coastal wetlands could be destroyed.

37

Forests

Global losses of forest area have marched in step with population growth for human history. The two trends rose slowly for millennia, turned upward in recent centuries, and accelerated sharply after 1900. Indeed, 75 per cent of the historical growth in global population and an estimated 75 per cent of the loss in global forested area have occurred in the twentieth century. The correlation makes sense, given the additional need for farmland, pastureland, and forest products as human numbers expand. But since 1950, the advent of mass consumption of forest products has quickened the pace of deforestation.

In some cases, population pressure is still closely linked with deforestation. In Latin America, for example, ranching is the single largest cause of deforestation. Because most meat produced in Latin America is consumed there, and because meat consumption per person has been largely unchanged for several decades, it is likely that expanding population is the principal reason for ranching-related deforestation. In addition, analysts at the World Resources Institute estimate that overgrazing and overcollection of firewood which are often a function of a growing population are degrading some 14 per cent of the world's threatened frontier forests (large areas of virgin forest). In fact, a U.N. Food and Agriculture Organisation study showed a one-to-one correlation between population growth and fuelwood consumption in 16 Asian countries between 1961 and 1994.

On the other hand, deforestation created by the demand for forest products tracks more closely with rising per capita consumption in recent decades, Global use of paper and paperboard per person, for example, has doubled (or nearly tripled) since 1961, and most of the increase has come in wealthy countries with low or even stable levels of population growth. Europe, Japan, and North America, with 16 per cent of global population, consume 63 per cent of the world's paper and paperboard and nearly half its industrial wood.

Although consumption and population growth have operated somewhat independently in the late twentieth century, the two forces could coincide in the developing world in coming decades, with substantial consequences for forests. Developing country paper consumption is less than one tenth the level found in industrial nations, suggesting that large increases in consumption are likely as these nations prosper. (It also suggests that greater economy is needed in industrial countries). With 80 per cent of the world's people, and as home to all the increase in population in coming decades, even modest growth in per capita paper and wood consumption in developing countries could place substantial pressure on forests. If paper were used by the entire world in 2050 at today's industrial-nation rates, paper production would need to jump more than eightfold over 1996 levels.

This projected growth is unsustainable, given that global use of forest products is already near or beyond the limits of sustainable use. Using data on sustainable forest yields, and assuming that virgin forests are left intact, researchers at Friends of the Earth UK have determined that production of forest products for the world is 25 per cent beyond the most restrictive estimates for sustainable consumption. (Many forests, of course, are already logged well beyond sustainable levels). The most optimistic assessment would allow for a further 35 per cent growth in consumption. Even that spells trouble, however, given a projected global population increase of some 54 per cent over the next half-century, and given the likely increase in consumption from rising prosperity. Lower consumption of forest products and increased recycling in industrial countries can make room for a more prosperous developing world to enjoy the products of the world's forests, but the task will be made easier if population growth everywhere is stabilized sooner rather than later.

If population and consumption eat into the world's forests, the resulting loss of forest services reduces, in turn, a country's capacity to support its population. Forests provide habitat to a diverse selection of wildlife; tropical forests, for example, are home to more than 50 per cent of the world's species. And as storehouses of carbon, forests are key to regulating climate. Deforestation leads to huge releases of carbon: an estimated one quarter of the world's carbon emissions come from forest clearing. Loss of these macroservices undermines the stability and resiliency of the global environment on which economies and populations depend. In addition, forests provide services vital to a local population, such as control of erosion, steady provision of water across rainy and dry seasons, and regulation of rainfall. Taken together, the loss of these services due to deforestation can upset local economies and subject local populations to economic instability.

38

Sustainable Tourism-illusion or Realistic Alternative?

We find them in the big cities of the world and in the most remote jungles; they cross the deserts of Africa and cruise to see the penguins along the polar ice caps: they climb the Himalayan mountains and dive deep into the coral seas of tropical oceans. Tourists are every where these days easily recongnisable by their cameras and camcorders, their leisure-time outfit, and their unsatiable desire to get away from home and experience life with a difference.

Tourism has become the biggest industry in the world. It offers jobs for 200 million people and contributes 11.7 per cent to global Gross National Product. Almost 700 million tourist arrivals are expected for this year, and this number is estimated to grow to 1.5 billion by the year 2020.

Most countries in he world, with very few exceptions, compete with each other to get as large a share as possible of the huge cake which is up for distribution. Attracting tourists, especially from beyond the own borders, means foreign exchange earnings and jobs and income for the local people. But the list of possible draw backs, especially for developing countries, is along: the environment and natural beauty may be harmed by infrastructure and hotel buildings: the intrusion of large numbers of foreigners with little knowledge and respect for the local culture and tradition may cause social tensions; there may be an upsurge of prostitution and sex-related diseases; and the local economy may be disrupted because labor is siphoned off from farming to the tourism sector, and the high purchasing power of tourists may promote inflation.

People concerned over these undesirable side-effects of tourism have, therefore, invented the term of 'soft' tourism—one which would impact less on the society and environment of the host country. The latest catchwords are' sustainable' tourism or 'eco-tourism' suggesting that tourism can be organised in such a way that it does not harm the environment and local culture. But are we not deceiving ourselves if we believe that tourism in its modern forms can be 'sustainable'? Sustainable according to the widely used definition of the Brundtlandt Commission means "meeting the needs of the present without compromising the ability of future generations to meet their own needs".

This entails, for instance, that we try to avoid the possible effects of climate change which is caused by greenhouse gas emissions into the atmosphere. Tourism because of the enormous increase in air and road traffic, is a major factor in polluting the atmosphere, increasing CO2 emissions, and damaging the protective ozone layer. Also, increased traffic as a result of tourism used up additional non-renewal resources such as petrol and kerosene and adds to air pollution in overcrowded cities or in frequented tourist regions. Needless to argue that the term "sustainable" could hardly be applied in this connection, especially in view of that fact that tourist numbers are going to double in the next 20 years.

Also tourism is by no means more 'sustainable' if tourist leave their ghettos and begin to interact with the local population. As long only a few open-minded people seek to submerge themselves in the culture and society of the host country this may lead to more interaction and inter-cultural understanding. But just imagine what would happen if all the Japanese and Americans visiting Paris, Rome or Berlin during the summer would come knocking at the door of local people to learn more about their real life. Or if all the Germans on the beaches of Thailand would decide that travelling with a backpack through the country's villages was more rewarding than staying in a luxurious hotel Then it would soon turn out that such a form of tourism was even less 'sustainable' than organised travel in its present form.

The only truly 'sustainable' form of tourism, therefore, would be to stay at home and to avoid additional resource consumption. For obvious reasons, this is no realistic alternative and, if consistently applied, would lead to a world economic crisis. Instead of using the illusionary term 'sustainable' tourism, we should, therefore, speak more often about 'responsible' tourism. This term implies that we try to keep the negative environmental and cultural impacts of tourism at a minimum while making sure that benefits go to the poor, especially in developing countries. 'Responsible' tourism is not against traveling, but it takes care that landscapes are not destroyed, natural and architectural beauties preserved, foreign cultures respected, and economic benefits spread as widely as possible. 'Responsible'tourism has the advantage that corresponds both to the wishes of most tourists who want to stay in a clean environment with a clean conscience and the interests of the local people who derive jobs and incomes from it. But it needs strong state which is able to enforce environmental regulations, suppress corruption and make sure that income from tourism benefits the whole country and not only a few national or international entrepreneurs.

To travel and to experience the world is an age-old dream which more and more people in the richer parts of the world are able to fulfil for themselves. But the tourism boom threatens to become self-destructive if it continues to expand without fetters. 'Responsible' tourism strikes a balance between the needs of the environment, the respect for the other culture, and the wish of modern people to live in a world without borders. However, it is an illusion to believe that mass tourism with 1.5 billion arrivals per year could truly be sustainable.

39

Forests:

The Earth's Lungs

The world's forest cover is shrinking. Over the past 50 years nearly half of the world's original forest cover has been lost—some 3 billion hectares. Each year another 16 million hectares of virgin forest are cut, bulldozed, or burned.

Between 1980 and 1995 the world lost some 180 million hectares of forest—an area the size of Indonesia. While developed countries had a net increase of 20 million hectares due to reforestation, this gain was more than offset by a net decrease of 200 million hectares in the developing world.

Forests have many functions of value both to humanity and to nature itself. Take away the trees, and the intricately linked ecosystem unravels. Forests absorb carbon dioxide and produce oxygen, anchor soils, regulate the water cycle, protect against erosion, and provide a habitat for millions of species.

Forest products are essential to the world economy, worth about US$400 billion annually in timber, pulp, paper, and fuel wood. Forest products other than wood, such as medicines, vegetables, and fruits, provide another US$20 billion and are growing in importance.

Healthy forests boost food production. Trees soak up and store water from season to season, slowly releasing moisture during dry periods. Without tree cover, water runs off faster during the tropical rainy season, carrying away valuable topsoil. A World Bank study found that the rate of soil loss was 10 times higher on forest lands where slash-and-burn shifting cultivation was practiced than in undisturbed forests.

One reason that agricultural yields have fallen in sub Sahran Africa is that vast amounts of forests cover have disappeared, hastening soil erosion and loss of soil nutrients.

Forest cover regulates climate, while destruction of forests contribute to global warning. Whereas living trees soak up and store carbon dioxide from the atmosphere trees that are cut down and burned release carbon into the atmosphere. In the last decade tropical deforestation has released large amounts of stored carbon—accounting for roughly one-quarter of the carbon dioxide emissions to the atmosphere due to human activity.

Pressures on Forests

Current demand for forests products may exceed the limits of sustainable consumption by 25 per cent. The developed world accounts for most of the demand for forest products. With just 16 per cent of the world's population, North America, Europe, and Japan consume two-thirds of the world's paper and paperboard and half its industrial wood. Demand for industrial wood products also has risen in developing countries, however, along with demand for fuel wood, the main energy source for many rural communities.

Throughout the 1990s many developing countries with rapid population growth had high rates of deforestation. Forest land was converted to agricultural use, and trees cut to provide housing and wood for fuel. Moreover developing countries stepped up exports of forests, products to meet the rising demand from developed countries.

The amount of forest area per capita fell by half between 1960 and 1995—reflecting both population growth and the disappearance of forests cover. In 1995 close to 1.7 billion people lived in countries with less than one-tenth of a hectare of forest cover per capita (83). By 2025, an estimated 4.6 billion people will live in such countries.

What Can Be Done?

As population grows and per capita consumption of forest products increases, countries must do more to manage forest resources on a sustainable basis. The following developments offer encouragement.

Technological Improvements

Technological improvements including use of recycled paper and paperboard, have substainally reduced the amount of pulp needed to produce paper. In 1970 paper and paperboard consisted of 80 per cent wood pulp. By 1997 more efficient production processes had reduced that figure to 56 per cent. As a direct result, the production of pulp for paper is expected to grow by just over 1 per cent a year over the next decade, about half the growth rate in the 1980s.

Forest Products Certification

Adopting a system that identifies forest products that come from sustainable managed forests could support efforts toward sustainability. As of 1998, about 10 million hectares of forest lands have been certified. Over 90 per cent of the certified area is in northern, temperature forests, mostly in Europe and North America. Close to 60 per cent of the entire certified area is in just two countries—Sweden and Poland—reflecting education and awareness campaigns in those countries. In tropical forests, where most of the destruction is taking place today, only tiny areas have been certified as providing sustainable yield.

Intergovernmental Responses

In 1995 the Intergovernmental Panel on Forests (IPF) was established in response to the 1992 Earth Summit. The IPF evolved into the inter governmental Forum on Forests in 1997, after the UN's five year review of the Earth Summit goals. The mission of the forum is to examine the underlying causes of deforestation and to help countries develop strategies that address them.

Efforts to advance an international legal convention on forests, which begin in 1990, have been shelved, however.

Some observers believe that advancing such a convention would only codify the standards of a weak consensus and thus would be worse than no convention at all. Widespread opposition to a convention makes it unlikely that the issues will reach the negotiating table.

Instead, many organisations urge governments of countries with large forest resources to enforce existing legislation and to introduce more effective forest conservation initiatives close to 130 countries have developed or updated their National Forest programmes over the past decade.

While such initiatives are promising, they cannot be expected to half forest destruction completely. Millions of people rely on forest products for their livelihoods. Sustainable forest management will require not just enforcement of laws that project forests but also alternative sources of livelihood for many rural people.

40

An Agenda for Change

The world's growing population, combined with unsustainable production and consumption patterns, is putting increasing stress on air, land, water, energy, and other essential resources.

- Development strategies will have to deal with the combination of population growth ecosystem health, technology, and access to resources. Meting the unmet need for family planning and reproductive health services should be part of national sustainable development strategies.

- The world needs to do a better job of forecasting the possible outcome of current human activities, including popualtion trends, per capita resource use, and wealth distribution.

Protecting the Atmosphere. The atmosphere is under increasing pressure from green house gases that threaten to change the climate and from chemicals that reduce the ozone layer. Governments need to:

- Modernize existing power system to gain energy efficiency and develop new and renewable energy sources.

- Promote national energy efficiency and emission standards and develop efficient, cost-effective, and less polluting mass transit systems.

Combating Deforestation. Forests world wide are threatened by uncontrolled degradation and conversion to other uses because of increasing human pressure.

- There is an urgent need to conserve and plant forests in developed and developing countries to maintain or restore the ecological balance and to provide for human needs.
- Governments need to work with business, scientists, local community groups, indigenous people, and the public to create long-term conservation and management policies for every forest region and watershed.

Sustainable Agriculture and Rural Development. Hunger is already a constant threat to over 800 million people, while the world's ability to continue meeting growing demand for food and other agricultural products over the long term is uncertain. Soil erosion, salinisation, water logging, and loss of soil fertility are increasing in all countries.

Agriculture has to meet rising needs mainly by increasing productivity, because most of the world's best croplands are already in use. At the same time further encroachment on land that is only marginally suitable for cultivation must be avoided.

- Sustainable agriculture and rural development will require major adjustments in agricultural, environmental, and economic policies in all countries and at the international level.

Conservation of Biological Diversity. The loss of the world's biological diversity continues, mainly from habitat destruction, over-harvesting, pollution, of foreign plants and animals (known and exotics). This decline in biodiversity is largely caused by human activity and represents a serious threat to our development.

- Develop national strategies to conserve and sustainably use biological diversity and to make these strategies part of overall national development efforts.
- Implement fair sharing of the benefits between providers and consumers of biological resources.

- Protect natural habitats. Promote the rehabilitation of damaged ecosystems.

Protecting and Managing the Oceans. Oceans are under increasing environmental stress from pollution over-fishing, and degradation of coastlines and coral reefs. About 70 per cent of marine pollution comes from sources on land. Countries should commit themselves to control and reduce degradation of the marine environment. They should:

- Build and maintain sewage treatment systems and avoid discharging sewage near shell fisheries, water intakes and bathing areas.
- Develop land-use practices that reduce run-off of soil and wastes to rivers and thus to the seas. Use environmentally less harmful pesticides and fertilizers.
- Control and prevent coastal erosion and silting due to land uses such as unplanned construction.

Protecting and Managing Fresh Water. In many parts of the world there is widespread scarcity, gradual destruction, and increased pollution of fresh water resources. The causes include the inadequately treated sewage and industrial waste, loss of natural water catchment areas, deforestation and other chemicals into the water. The following approaches are key:

- The way to provide all people with potable water and basic sanitation is to adopt the approach "some for all rather than more for some." This approach can be achieved through low-cost services built and maintained at the community level.
- Nations need to identify and protect water resources and see that water is used on a sustainable basis. They need effective water pollution prevention and control programmes. There is a particular need for appropriate sanitation and waste-disposal technologies for low-income, high-density cities.

41

Global Warming:
Worrisome Signs

Scientists increasingly agree that the earth's atmosphere is becoming warmer. A long-term rise in the global climate could cause sea levels to rise around the world and bring a number of other adverse consequences. Reliance on fossil fuels as an energy source and the widespread destruction and burning of forests are chiefly responsible for the carbon emissions, the so-called greenhouse gases that lie behind global warming.

One indication of global warming is that over the past 40 years the ocean surface (the top 1,000 feet) has warmed an average of half a degree Celsius. The US National Oceanic and Atmospheric Administration (NOAA) has reported that tropical waters in the Northern Hemisphere have been warming up even faster—in fact, 10 times faster than the measured global rate—because tropical oceans retain heat more readily than other areas.

Rising Sea Levels

Studies project that by 2100 the earth's surface temperature could increase between 1.0 and 3.5 degrees Celsius. If the highest projection were reached, Greenland's ice sheet probably would melt. As a consequence, the global sea level gradually would rise as much as seven metres.

Computer models project that this rise in sea level would take more than a millennium. Some climatologists, however, think that sea levels could rise much faster, pointing to dramatic shrinkage of the Arctic ice cap over the past 30 years.

Even a rise of one metre in sea level which could occur by 2080, according to the computer models would inundate many low-lying coastal areas around the world. For instance, much of the Nile River Delta of Egypt would disappear. A one-metre rise in global sea levels also would inundate close to 20 per cent of the coastline of Bangladesh and displace millions of people.

Adverse Health Effects

Rising global temperatures also would carry adverse health consequences. As temperatures warmed and episodes of droughts and floods became more frequent, the incidence of water-borne diseases and a resurgence and spread of infectious diseases carried by mosquitoes and other disease vectors probably would increase.

Warmer global temperatures also would magnify the effects of human activities on the environment, including more pollution and habitat destruction. Climate change might even cause some ecosystems to exceed critical thresholds, leading to their irreversible decline.

Growing Scientific Consensus

In 1988, to help study and focus attention on the issues, the Intergovernmental panel on climate change was created under the auspices of the World Meteorological Organisation and the United Nations Environment programme. The panel has involved as many as 2000 scientists from around the world. In 1996 a panel report concluded firmly that global climate change is a reality and not just a possibility. After reviewing the evidence, the panel determined that:

- Evidence for the link between climate change and human activities is compelling. Already, increases in carbon dioxide and other climate changing gases have upset the balance of the earth and its atmosphere.
- The earth's surface has become warmer; the number and severity of storms have increased; and the global

sea level has risen by 10-25 cm. over the past century.

Because the warming trend is a global problem, solutions must be global in scope, the panel concluded.

Why is the Climate Changing

Over the last 150 years burning of fossil fuels has released some 270 billion tons of carbon into the atmosphere in the form of heat-trapping carbon dioxide gases. Since 1950 annual worldwide carbon emission have increased fourfold, reaching 6.3 billion tons in 1997. Other emissions that contribute to climate change include methane (mainly from domestic livestock and agriculture), nitrous oxide, and chlorofluorocarbons.

Atmospheric concentrations of carbon dioxide reached 363 parts per million in 1998, the highest level since the time of massive volcanic activity over 160,000 years ago, based on examiantion of ice cores in Antarctica and in the Arctic. If current trends continue, atmospheric concentrations of carbon dioxide would double during this century.

About three-fourths of the huge increase in carbon emissions over the past half-century is due to increased energy consumption per capita; about one-quarter is due to population growth. Western industrialized countries account for nearly half of atmospheric carbon emissions, but developing countries are producing a growing share as industrial activity increases and populations grow. China is now the world's second largest carbon emitter, after the US.

Vanishing Carbon Sinks

The earth's forests are carbon sinks that currently soak up an estimated one-third of the carbon dioxide released into the atmosphere. When forests burn, whether naturally or when people clear the land, they not only release more carbon into the atmosphere but also diminish the amount of carbon-absorbing forest cover remaining.

Some scientists are concerned that droughts caused by global warming will increase the number of forest fires, thus contributing further to carbon emissions in the atmosphere. For instance, the six months of extensive forest fires that occurred in Asia in 1997 and 1998 released more carbon into the atmosphere than western Europe emits in a year. Burning trees for land clearance in the tropics releases about 1 billion tons of carbon into the atmosphere annually.

As more carbon fills the atmosphere, scientists worry that forests will become saturated and no longer play their role as carbon sinks. Instead, they will start to release carbon themselves.

Agriculture at Risk

Higher carbon dioxide levels in the atmosphere would extend the agricultural growing season and promote forest growth in the short run but would have potentially negative effects on crops and forests in the long run. Because the world's grain belts would become less productive, an additional 350 million people would go hungry by the middle of this century. Major droughts have been projected for sub-Saharan Africa as climatic patterns shift, reducing rainfall and drying out soils for longer periods.

In 1999 NOAA project that by the middle of this century soils in agricultural regions of the Central US, Central Asia, and the areas surrounding the Mediterranean Sea would likely experience substantial reductions in soil moisture during the summer growing season because evaporation rates would be higher. Such reductions in soil moisture would make these areas particularly vulnerable.

Others point out that, ironically, global warming could produce colder temperatures in Northern Europe and Russia, reducing crop yields in these regions as well. This change would occur because the huge amounts of arctic fresh water from melting ice caps would make the water less dense. Such a change would interrupt the "conveyor belt" effect of the North Atlantic Drift, the ocean current that transports warm tropical water from the Gulf Stream to Scandinavia and Northern Europe.

What Can be Done?

What is the prospect for reducing emissions of carbon dioxide into the atmosphere? The United Nations Framework Convention on Climate change was opened for signature at the Rio Earth summit in 1992. It was promptly signed and ratified by most low-lying island states and countries with extensive coastal areas. The Convention established a framework and a process for agreeing on specific actions later on; it asked signatory states to take preliminary action to reduce greenhouse gas emissions; and it encouraged scientific research on climate change.

42

Ecosystems, Our Unknown Protectors

How ecosystems work and what part they play in biodiversity remain a mystery. But we do know that they perform a host of invaluable services for the human species. In my view, biodiversity's fundamental value is neither aesthetic nor economic but environmental, even though most people are largely unaware of this. The value of biodiversity is often measured in terms of the number of species living in a given area. But the interactions between the many species in an ecosystem, and between them and the environment's physical and chemical components are also very important. This highly intricate web of relationships makes an ecosystem more valuable than the sum of the species it contains.

Ecosystems perform services that are essential for the survival of the human species. They fix carbon in the atmosphere and produce oxygen, protect soil from erosion and keep it fertile, filter water and replenish aquifers, provide pollination and anti-parasite agents and so on.

The first two of these services are closely related to each other. They result from photosynthesis, whereby green plants, starting with algae, absorb carbon dioxide (CO_2) and emit oxygen. For millions for years, the balance between the various gases in the atmosphere remained stable. But with the coming of the industrial revolution, humans began burning increase amounts of fossil fuels. Today, three billion tonnes of carbon build up in the atmosphere each year and natural ecosystems can no longer absorb all these emissions—especially since they are disappearing at an alarming rate.

Deforestation alone releases such tremendous amounts of CO_2 and other gases, such as methane, that it has become the second-leading cause of global warming.

Storing freshwater, protecting soil and keeping it fertile are three other closely related functions. Ecosystems are veritable "freshwater factories". They absorb rainwater and slowly filter it through the soil before draining it towards streams, rivers, lakes and underground aquifers that supply us with the precious liquid. When the vegetal ground cover is degraded, the water cycle is disrupted. Rain strikes the bare earth, washing away huge amounts of nutritional substances. Reservoirs, lakes and rivers silt up.

Uncertain Reaction to Climate Change

Despite years of research, scientists still know very little about how ecosystems work. We are generally incapable of predicting how they will react to certain transformations in the environment, especially climate changes. Nor do we know any more about whether a species present in a given environment is superfluous or "replicable", even when it is very rare. Likewise, we do not know which key species are indispensable to maintaining an ecosystem, with a few exceptions such as pine forests, where that tree is obviously the dominant species.

We know even less about the part biological diversity itself play in maintaining ecosystems and the services they perform. One simple example is a highest diversified forest that absorbs carbon dioxide—a vital function, as we have seen, for limiting global warming. Suppose the forest is cleared to make way for a single-crop forest. The service will still be performed, perhaps even better at first because young, fast-growing trees absorb more CO_2 than old ones, which regenerate slowly. But what will happen in the long term? After several decades, the consequences of the loss of biodiversity will probably be felt. Replacing many species with a single one will have certainly depleted the soil and, in the long term, slowed down the forest's growth and consequently its ability to absorb CO_2.

More generally, diversified ecosystems seem more productive. Specialists remain wary about their conclusions, but today they believe that biodiversity helps ecosystems to resist alien species and diseases and to recover faster in the event of disruption. In the face of doubt, and to find out more about them, it is better to preserve as many different ecosystems as possible.

A Costly Lesson for New York City

Most people take it for granted that ecosystems will carry on performing services without receiving anything in return. They think nature will continue benefiting humanity, no matter how much damage is done. The survival of organisms other than our own species is perceived as a frill that future generations can live without.

These preconceived ideas are wrong and dangerous as the city of New York has recently come to realize. The city's water has always enjoyed such a good reputation that it was sold throughout the northeastern United States. Its equality was due to Catskill Mountains' natural purification system. But that ecosystem has suffered so much from pollution, especially fertilizer run-off from farms, that by the late 1990s New York's water had become undrinkable. The city planned to build a purification plant, whose cost was put at between six and eight billion dollars, not including the $300 million in yearly operating costs—an astronomical bill for a service that had always been free! The price was so staggering that the city eventually decided to restore the Catskill Mountains' degraded environment at a cost of only one billion dollars.

This story clearly illustrates where our interests lie. We must preserve ecosystems and the conditions that enable our planet to ensure the survival of *Homo sapiens* or, at least, the short-term maintenance of our current quality of life.

43

Using Economics to Advantage

In the eyes of the public, the economic sectors for instance energy, transport and agriculture are often seen as pursuing interests that conflict with environment and health. They are the originators of pollution and often devise economic arguments to oppose change in their practice that could improve environment and health. This behaviour has led the public, as well as environment and health professionals, to view economic analysis negatively. However, these economic arguments are often inadequate and unconvincing from the point of view of many economists.

In fact, the economic rationale is bound to reflect as closely as possible the preferences of the population and thus to take much greater account of environment and health. If used by environment and health authorities, economic analysis can be turned into a powerful tool for supporting their policies.

Why use Economics?

First, economies can help to make explicit the benefits of environmental health improvements and the costs of the impacts. This provides additional arguments to encourage decision-makers to integrate environment and health considerations in their policies.

Second, current prices rarely reflect the full environment and health costs of the production or consumption of goods and services. Therefore, producers and customers have no economic reasons to reduce the impact they have on environment and health, as they do not pay prices that reflect this impact. Nor are they encouraged to take it into account in their investment decisions and lifestyle choices.

This could be corrected by reflecting as much as possible environment and health costs in the prices. Economic instruments such as environmental taxes or tradable permits are a promising solution. A first step in that direction is the removal of subsidies that support practices harmful to the environment and health. In most of the cases, however, it would be difficult to remove decorative subsidies immediately and charge the full amount of environment and health costs. Nevertheless, negotiating plans and timetables to do so progressively, is a strong signal to the economic actors. It modifies their anticipation of future prices, as they know they will have to pay in the future for the environment and health costs they will create. This drives them increasingly to design their long-term choices and strategies in an environment-friendly way.

Finally, the setting of new economic instruments is usually under the responsibility of the Ministry of Finance. It also implies negotiations with economic sectors. Therefore environment and health authorities will need to play a more pro-active role in order to advance the integration of environmental health in sectoral and economic policies. Success will depend on their ability to discuss and present economic arguments in support of environmental health considerations.

A Promising Initiative

The present situation is that many environment and health authorities have few skills in using economic arguments and that economic sectors very often continue to ignore environment and health considerations.

International organisation-will also be invited to strengthen their co-operation in environment and health economics. In order to sustain the policy changes, promoting environment and health, co-operative efforts will aim.

- To support the development of the capacities of the environment and health authorities to use economic analysis;
- To improve the focus on health outcomes in national or inter-country processes dealing with environment and health issues. This will include the contribution of health expertise in these processes and the use of economic arguments to greater advantage;
- To exchange information early in the planning process of their respective programmes that use economic tools for addressing environment and health.
- To further co-ordinate their current and future activities in support of environment and health.

44

Myths and Illusions

The ride of precarity is rising steadily, so that people who have never been poor no longer regard poverty as a distant prospect but as one so close that it could engulf them at any moment.

In 1989, the fall of the Berlin Wall was rightly welcomed because it marked the collapse of a system that provided a degree of equality but rejected freedom. Today there is a strong possibility that the system gradually spreading all over the world—a kind of neo-liberal fundamentalism—may also collapse. In its obsession with freedom, vital though freedom is, this fundamentalism disregards equality, a term, which should not be, regarded here in purely static and statistical terms, but as something dynamic and ethical. Equality can only be truly practiced in a context of social solidarity or to borrow from the vocabulary of the French Revolution of fratemity.

On the one hand we have a world that is immensely rich in resources, possibilities, knowledge and experience; its constituent societies are freer and more dynamic than ever. There is an extraordinary potential to everyone to live a better life. But at the same time, new and ever higher wall are being built both between peoples and between social groups within individual countries. We are experiencing a travesty of development, which is creating a world bipolarized into extremes of wealth and poverty.

The most common reactions to this disastrous situation are very often the result of two misapprehensions. The first can only be described as ideological or doctrinaire since it is not based on the facts as they can be observed. It says that since the dominant system of values and things is by definition more than satisfactory, the persistence of impoverishment is merely a temporary blip. Enough time has elapsed, however, for us to see that this is not the case, including in countries where this system has been part of the established order for more than a century. One statistic is particularly eloquent. In just over 30 years, world production has approximately doubled, but the gap has more than doubled between the income of the 20 per cent of world's people living in the richest countries and the income of the world's poorest 20 per cent, according to the United Nations Development Programmes.

The second misapprehension stems from another form of blindness and illusion, namely the belief that poverty can be regarded exclusively as a moral issue, as if it had no other kind of implications for those who are not poor. Globalisation is, however, a two-way process. It enable the countries of the North to export their values and their paradigms as well as their goods and capital to the countries of the South, but it also makes them much more vulnerable to the backlash of crises that afflict these countries. Even in the North, the cult of competitiveness is undermining situations once considered extremely stable. The tide of precarity is rising steadily, so that people who have never been poor no longer regard poverty as a distant prospect but as one so close that it could engulf them at any moment.

Because of inadequate socio-economic development, the extraordinary upsurge of democracy over the past 30 years remains a very fragile process, and there is a risk that the trend may be reversed. When hunger, disease and ignorance prevail, citizens' participation in decision-making becomes either non-existent or a mere charade. Democratic institutions become empty shells, representational bodies existing in form only and devoid of real significance

Social divisions caused by economic distortions exacerbate the failures of democracy which in turn pose serious threats to civil order within countries and to peace between nations. It is high to face these obvious facts.

Bibliography

Books

A. C. Pigou (1960). *The Economics of Welfare*, Macmillan & Co. Ltd., London.

Ahluwalia Montek, S. (1985). *Rural Poverty, Agricultural Production and Prices: A Re-Examination* in John Mellor and Desai Gunvant, M. (eds.) "Agricultural Changes and Rural Poverty", The John Hopkins University Press, London.

Amartya Sen (1995). *The Hindu*, 6th November, Interviewed by Ramamanohar Reddy, Chennai.

Betellei, A. (2000). *Chronicles of Over Time*, Penguine Books, New Delhi.

Carr, Maryn et al., (1997). Speaking Out; *Women's Economic Empowerment in South Asia,* Vikas Publications, New Delhi.

Chakravarthy Sukamoy (1989). *Development Planning, The Indian Experience*, Oxford University Press, New Delhi.

Char ly, S. R. and G. K. Karanth (1998). *Challenging Untouchability, Dalit Initiative and Experience from Karnataka*, Sage Publications, New Delhi.

Chinnadurai, K. (1986). *Evaluation Study of Implementation* of IRDO, State Bank of India, Coimbatore.

Dantwala, M. L. (1996). *Dilemmas of Growth*: the Indian Experience, Sagar Publications; New Delhi.

Delige R. (1999). *The Untouchables of India*, Berg, New York.

Desai, B. M. and N. V. Namboodiri (1993). *Rural Financial Institutions: Promotion and Performance*, Oxford and IBH Publishing Company Pvt. Ltd., New Delhi.

Dev, S. Mahendra (1999). *State Interventions and Women's Employment*, in T. S. Papola and Alakh N. Sharma (Eds) (1999). "Gender and Employment in India"; Vikas Publishing House Pvt. Ltd., New Delhi, pp. 373-411.

Dharm Narain & Sen, A. K. et al. (1989). *Studies on Indian Agriculture*, Oxford University Press, New Delhi.

Frencine Fournier (1997). *Foreword, Poverty and Participation in Civil Society*. Edited by Yogesh Atal of Else Oyen, Abhinav Publications, New Delhi.

George Psacharopoulos and Moureen Woodhall (1986). *Education for Development; An, Analysis of Investment Choices,* Oxford, New York.

Griffin (1979). *The Political Economy of Agrarian Change,* The MacMillan Press Ltd., London.

Griffin Keith (1978). *International Inequality and National Poverty,* The Macmillan Press Ltd., London.

Griffin Keith (1981). *Land Concntration and Rural Poverty,* The Macmillan Press Ltd., Hong Kong.

Gunnar Myrdal (1968). *Asian Drama—An Inquiry into Poverty of Nations,* Pantheon, New York.

Gunnar Myrdal (1970). *The Challenge of World Poverty, A World Anti-Poverty Programme in Outline,* Pantheon, New York.

Gupta, D. (2000). *Interrogating Caste: Understanding Heirarchy and Difference in Indian Society,* Penguine Books, New Delhi.

Haq, Mahabub Ul. (1978). *The Poverty Curtain: Choices for the Third World,* Oxford University Press, Bombay.

Haq, Mahabub Ul. (1997). *Human Development in South Asia,* Oxford University Press, New York.

Harper, M. (1998). *"Profit for the Poor"*, Oxford and IBH Publishing Co., Delhi.

Hirway Indira (1984). *Programmes for Poverty Eradication: A Critique of Target Group Approach,* Sardar Patel Institute for Economic and Social Research (Mimeo).

Holcombe, Susan(1995). *Managing to Empower; The Grameena Bank's Experience of Poverty Alleviation*, Oxford University Press Dhaka.

IFMR (1984). *An Economic Assessment of Poverty Eradication and Rural Unemployment Alleviation Programme and their Prospects,* Madras.

Jackson Dudley (1972). *Poverty, MacMillan Studies in Economics,* MacMillan, London.

Karmakar, K. G. (1999). *Rural Credit and Self-Help Groups, Micro-Finance Needs and Concepts in India*. Sage Publications, New Delhi.

Kaushik Dasu (1984). *The Development Economy: A Critique of Contemporary Theory,* Oxford University Press, Delhi.

Khan Azizur Rahman & Eddy Lee (1984). *Poverty in Rural Asia,* Asian Employment Programme (ARTEP), International Labour Organisation, Bangkok, Thailand.

Kuznets S. (1965). *Economic Growth and Structure,* Heinemann, London.

Lewis, A. (1966). *Developmnet Planning,* Allen & Unwin, London.

Mahammad Haan Khan (1981). *Underdevelopment and Agrarian Structure in Pakistan,* A West View Replica Edition, West View Press, U.S.A.

Maheswari, S. R.(1985). *Rural Development in India,* Sage Publications, Delhi.

Minhas R. S. (1974). *Planning and the Poor,* S. Chand & Company Limited, New Delhi.

Mukta Mittal (1995). *Women Power in India,* Anmol Publications Pvt. Ltd., New Delhi.

Myrdal Gunner (1968). *Asian Drama, Volume-III,* Twentieth Century Fund, New York.

NABARD (1999). *Banking with the Poor: Financing Self-help Groups,* CGM, NABARD, Hydreabad.

NABARD (1999-2000). *NABARD and Micro-finance,* Mumbai.

Nanda, Y.C. (2000). *Role of Banks in Rural Development in the New Millennium, National Bank for Agriculture and Rural Development,* Mumbai.

NCERT (2000). *Human Development in South India,* Oxford, New Delhi.

Parthasarathy, G. (1982). *Integrated Rural Development Concepts, Theoretical Base and Contradiction, in* "Development Planning and Policy", Edited by Gupta D.B., et al., Wiley Eastern, New Delhi.

Rahman, Hossain Zillus (1998). *Poverty Issues in Bangladesh,* Power and Participation Research Centre, Mimeo.

Rai & Tandon (1999). *Voluntray Development Organisation and Socio-economic Development,* Indian Economic Association, 82th Conference Volume, Amritsar.

Sakuntala Narasimhan (1999). *Empowering Women, An Alternative for Strategy from Rural India,* Sage Publications, New Delhi.

Sen A. K. (1984). Poverty and Famines: *An Essay on Entitlement and Deprivation,* Oxford University Press, Delhi.

Shylendra, H.S. (1999). *Promoting Women's Self-help Groups; Lessons from an Action Research Project of IRMA,* Anand, India, Working Paper No. 121.

The World Bank (2000-2001). *World Development Report,* Oxford, New York.

Todaro Michael, P. (1977). *Economics for a Developing World,* Longmans, London.

Todaro Michael, P. (1990). *Economics for a Developing World,* Second Edition, Longman, New York.

Von Braun, J., Bayes, F. and Akhter, R. (1999). *Village Pay Phones and Poverty Reduction. ZEF Discussion Papers on Development Policy No. 18,* Centre for Development Research, University of Barlin.

Von Pischke, J. D. et al. (1983) *Rural Financial Markets in Developing Countries: Their Use and Abuse,* John Hopkins University, Baltimore, U. S.A.

Yogesh Atal (1996). *Poverty and Participation in Civil Society,* Abhinav Publications, New Delhi.

Zeller, Manfred and Manohar Sharma (1998). *Rural Finance and Poverty Alleviation,* Food Policy Report, International Food Policy Research Institute, Washington DC, USA.

Journals

Amitava Mukherjee (1999). *Out of the abysis. The Challenge Confronting Some Civil Society Actors,* Indian Economic Association, 82 Conference, Amritsar.

Awasthi, P. K., et al., (1986). 'IRDP: Receptivity and Reaction', *Indian Journal of Agricultural Economics,* Vol. 41, No.4, October-December.

Bagchee Sandeep (1987). 'Poverty Alleviation Programmes in Seventh Plan: An Appraisal', *Economic and Political Weekly,* Vol. XXII, No. 4, January 24.

Bardhan, P K. (1973). On the Incidence of Poverty in Rural India of the Sixties, *Economic and Political Weekly,* February.

Bhat, Mazi, P. N. and et al., (1999). *Finding of National Family Health Survey, Regional Analysis, Economic and Political Weekly, Vol. XXXIV, Nos. 42 and 43,* Oct. 16-22/23-29.

Chambers, Robert (1994). *"Poverty and Livelihoods: Whose Reality Counts?" Overview Paper II, UNDP Stockholm Roundtable,* "Change: Social Conflict or Harmony?" 22-24 July.

Copertake Jemes G. (1996). *The Resilience of IRDP: Reform and Perpetuation of an Indian Myth. Development Policy Review,* 14

Dantwala, M. L. (1983). 'Rural Development: Investment Without Organisation', *Economic and Political Weekly.*

Desai, A. R. (1987). 'Rural Development and Human Rights in Independent India, *Economic and Political Weekly,* Vol. XXII, No. 31.

Desai, B.M. and J.W. Mellor (1993). *Institutional Fiance for Agricultural Development: An Analytical Survey of Critical Issues, Food Policy Review I,* International Food Policy Research Institute, Washinton, DC, USA.

Ghosh, D.K. (1995). *Group Cohesiveness in DWCRA Groups: An Application of Sociometric Approach,* Kurukshetra, May-June.

Govil, R.K. (1982). 'Micro-Level Planning and Rural Development', *Kurukshetra.*

Grewal, R.S. *et al.,* (1985). 'Impact of Integrated Rural Development Programme on Rural Women in Bhiwani District of Haryana', *Indian Journal of Agricultural Economics,* Vol. XL, No. 3, July-September.

Hare Gopal, G. & Balaramulu, Ch. 'Poverty Alleviation Programmes: IRDP in an Andhra Pradesh District, *Economic and Political Weekly,* Vol. XXIV, Nos. 35 & 36, September 2-9.

Hirway Indira (1984). *Programmes for Povety Eradication: A Critique of Target Group Approach,* Sardar Patel Institute for Economic and Social Research (Mimeo).

Jain, S.C. (1986). 'Poverty Alleviation Programmes in India: Some Issues of Micro Policy', *Indian Journal of Agricultural Economics,* Vol. XLI, No. 3, Conference Number, July-September.

Karmakar, K.G. (1999). *Rural Credit and Self-Help Groups; Micro-Finance Needs and Concepts in India,* Sage Publications, New Delhi.

Kumar Rajinder, *et al.,* (1986). 'Impact of Credit on Income, Employment and Capital Formulation of Rural Poor', *Indian Journal of Agricultural Economics,* Vol. 41, No.4, October-December.

M.S. Kallur (2001). *Empowerment of Women through NGOs: A Case Study of MYRADA Self-Help Groups,* Indian Journal of Agricultural Economics, Vol. 56, No.3.

Mosley, P. and R.P. Dahal (1985). *"Lending to the Poorest: Early Lessons from the Small Farmers: Development Programme, Nepal Development Policy Review,* Vol. 3, No. 2.

NIRD (1985). 'Employment and Income Generation Through IRDP, NREP and DRM', *Journal of Rural Development,* Vol. 4, No. 5, March-September.

Owusu, K. Opoku and William Tetteh (1982). *"An Experiment in Agricultural Credit: The Small Farmer Group Lending Programme in Ghana", Savings and Development,* Vol. 1, No. 1.

Rajaram Das Gupta (2001). *Working and Impact of Rural Self-Help Groups and Other Forms of Micro Financing, Indian* Journal of Agricultural Economics, Vol. 56, No.3.

Rajasekhar, D. (1996), *"Problems and Prospects of Group Lending in NGO Credit Programme in India", Saving and Development,* Vol. 20, No.1.

Sinha, S.P. & Prasad Jagadish (1980). 'Special Programmes for Weaker Sections: An Evaluation', *Indian Journal of Agricultural Economics,* Vol. XXXV, No. 4.

Stiglitz, J.E. (1990) *"Paper Monitoring and Credit Markets",* The World Bank Economic Review, Vol. 4, No. 3.

Thakur, D.S. (1977). 'Rural Development in India: Past Experience and Tasks Ahead', *Indian Journal of Agricultural Economics,* Vol. XXXII, No. 3, July-September.

The Hindu 2002, 11th May 2002, Chennai.

Yaron, J. (1992). *Successful Rural Finance Institutions,* World Bank Discussion Paper, 150, Washington, DC, USA.

Reports

Amitava Mukherjee (1999). *Out of the Abysis, The Challenge Confronting Some Civil Society Actors,* Indian Economic Association, 82 Conference, Amritsar.

APDPIP (2002), *On Andhra Pradesh District Poverty Initiatives Project Appraisal Document (PAD), Report No. 20089,* South Asia Regional Office.

Chief Planing Officer (2002). *Hand Book of Statistics, Mahabubnagar District,* Mhabubnagar.

Chief Planning Officer Collectorate (2000). *Hand Book of Statistics, Krishna District,* Machilipatnam.

Chief Planning Officer Collectorate (2001). *Hand Book of Statistics, Chittoor District,* Chittoor.

CIRDAP (1998). *Increased Household Income and Rural Women in Asia, Impact on Status and Activities,*, Dhaka, Bangladesh.

CIRDAP (1998). *Poverty Gender and Participation,* Dhaka.

CIRDAP (1999). *Rural Development Report, Centre on Integrated Rural Development for Asia and Pacific,* Dhaka.

CIRDAP (2000). *Poverty Gender and Participation,* Dhaka.

CMIE (2000). *Profile of Districts, Economic Intelligence Service,* October, Mumbai.

Government of Andhra Pradesh (1998). *Annual Report of the Commission of the Rural Development,* Hyderabad.

Government of Andhra Pradesh (1999). *Annual Report of the Commission of the Rural Development,* Hyderabad.

Government of Andhra Pradesh (1999). *New Series on State Domestic Product,* A.P., Hyderabad.

Government of Andhra Pradesh (2001). *Provisional Population Totals, Series 29,* Hyderabad.

Government of Andhra Pradesh (2001). *Statistical Abstract,* Hyderabad.

Government of Andhra Pradesh (2001). *Strategy Paper,* Hyderabad.

Government of India (1991). *Census of India,* New Delhi.

Government of India (1997-2002). *IX Five Year Plan,* New Delhi.

Government of India (2001), *Provisional Population Totals,* New Delhi.

Government of India (1974). *Towards Equality—Committee on the Status of Women in India.*

Government of India (1998, 99), *Reports of the Commissioner of SC and STs,* New Delhi.

Haq. Mahbub Ul. (1997). *Human Development in South Asia,* Oxford University Press, New York.

Holcombe, Susan (1995). *Managing to Empower. The Grameen Banks' Experience of Poverty Alleviation,* Oxford University Press, Dhaka.

IFAD (1996). *The State of World Poverty, Rome for a Discussion on the Process and Structural Causes of Poverty,* See Rovert Chambers (1983). Rural Development, Putting the Last First London, Longmans, One of the Best Discussions on how these Perpetuate Poverty.

IFAD (2001). *Rurual Poverty Report. The Challenge of Ending Rural Poverty,* Oxford, New York.

Indian Bank (2002-2003). *Annual Credit Plant, Krishna District (A.P.), Vijayawada.*

International Fund for Agricultural Development (IFAD) (1992). *The State World Rural Poverty—An Inquiry Into its Causes and Consequences,* New York University Press, New York.

ISACPA (1992). *Independent South Asia Commission for Poverty Alleviation.*

NABARD (1999). *Annual Report,* Mumbai.

NABARD (2000). *Annual Report,* Mumbai.

NABARD (2001). *Annual Report,* Mumbai.

NIRD (1994). *Rurual Development Report; Rural Employment,* Hyderabad, Andhra Pradesh.

NIRD (2001). *National Conference on SHG Movement in the Country & Swarnajanyanti Gram Swarozgar Yojana (SGSY), National Institute of Rural Development,* Hyderabad.

PEO (1985). *Evaluation Report on Integrated Rural Development Programme,* New Delhi.

RBI (1984). *Implementation of Integrated Rural Development Programme—* A Field Study.

SAARC (1992). *The Independent Source Asian Commission of the SAARC on Poverty Alleviation,* Dhaka.

South Asian Association for Regional Cooperation (SAARC) (1992). *Meeting the Challenge, Report of the Independent South Asian Commission on Poverty.*

The World Bank (1990). *World Development Report* Oxford, New York.

The World Bank (1991). *Gender and Poverty in India,* Washington DC.

The World Bank (1999-2000). *World Development Report 1999-2000,* Oxford University Press, New York.

UNDP (1994). *Human Development Report,* Oxford, New York.

UNDP (1996). *Human Development Report,* Oxford, New York.

UNDP (1997). *Human Development Report,* Oxford, New York.

UNDP (2000). *Human Development Report,* Oxford, New York.

World Bank (1990). *World Development Report—Poverty,* Oxford University Press.

Yerramaraju, B. and Firdausi, A.A. (1995). *Evaluation of DWCRA in Prakasam District,* Sponsored by Government of Andhra Pradesh, Administrative Staff College of India, Hyderabad.

Others

Government of Andhra Pradesh, Vision-2020, Hyderabad.

Government of India (1985). *Five Year Plan Documents (The Seventh and Eighth Five Year Plans 1985-95,* New Delhi, The Planning Commission).

NABARD (1984). *Study of Implementation of IRDP (Mimeo),* Bombay.

Government of Andhra Pradesh (1999). *Vision—2020,* Hyderabad, India.

Government of Andhra Pradesh, *Guidelines for Swarnajayanti Gram Swarozgar Yojana. Panchayati Raj and Rural Development Department,* Hyderbad.

IXth 5th Year Plan (1997-2000).

The Hindu (2002). April 27, Chennai.

The Hindu (2002). *Vision—2020.*

Index

F

L

M

N

O

P

V

W

Z